The Big Glow:
Insight, Inspiration, Peace and Passion

Brian Piergrossi

ISBN 978-1-4357-1228-7

Printed in the United States of America.

"If the only prayer you ever say your entire life is 'Thank you' that should suffice."
-Meister Eckhart

Thank you to every single person who has
ever been a part of my life,
For better or for worse,
And those that will arrive in the future.
This book would not have come into being
without you
This book is dedicated to YOU

TABLE OF CONTENTS:

VI: SUNSET..........144

I: TIMELESS

1- The Journey

We are about to take a journey together. You don't need to bring anything except your heart. All our primary needs will be provided for us as we go.

As you read these words, and we begin this journey, it is important to understand that you are not going to be the same person. We are embarking on a journey together that is going to change your life. It is my intention that it changes your life for the better. If your intention is the same, that is exactly what is going to happen. Life is simple that way.

Some books are eight-lane highways, which you speed through as fast as you can to accumulate the desired information. This is not that kind of journey and this is not that kind of book. This book contains no important information in it at all.

The intention of this book is not to provide you with new knowledge that will give you fulfillment, but rather to remove the clutter of knowledge that is preventing you from seeing it right now.

This is book is like a small explosion, opening up the heart and mind and flooding with renewed inspiration and passion. It is a practice in meditation and mindfulness. It is an exercise in attentive awareness to the wonder of the present moment. It is a testament to the fact that there is no moment more amazing than the one we are sharing right now.

This journey does not take place on an eight-lane highway, but rather like a small, quaint trail made by my own bare feet, meandering through a beautifully forested hilltop, with a vast, blue ocean down below and graceful dolphins undulating through the water.

As we become completely engrossed in the beauty of each tender step, we realize we don't need a destination. There is no goal and therefore there is no rush or hurry to get there. We are taking our time. The goal is within each step and this moment is the destination. Look closely! Don't pass by too quickly! There is beauty all around you.

This is not fast food, but should be cooked at a slow simmer for best taste and digestibility. There will be many points on this journey when you desire more time to fully digest and process what you read and what it means for you personally. You may read one sentence, one word, and not need to come back to this book for weeks! Take the necessary time you need.

This book is best read, if you are able, in the fresh, open air with the sky as your only roof. It is from here this book was inspired and it is here this book is most potent, inspiring and transformative.

Next to a lake in the morning sun
Underneath a big oak tree in the afternoon shade
By a powerful, rolling river
In a meadow, filled with wildflowers,
At a secluded beach, filled with the sounds of the rolling ocean
Sitting at sunset, with your back resting against a big, snow-capped mountain
In the silent, open desert, underneath a million twinkling stars in the vast, evening sky.

Read wherever and whenever you are able, and give each word and image your deepest attention.

This is a book, and a journey, you can come back to for inspiration, insight, passion and peace throughout the span of your life. Different portions of the book may be personal sources of inspiration at different times, depending upon the context of your current life circumstances and perspective.

2- The Intentions

This journey is unique in its structure
The intention of this book is to transmit a new way of perceiving the world and not a specific piece of knowledge.

It is filled with poems, prose, essays, stories, humor, aphorisms and questions separated into 333 pieces and 7 different chapters covering the span of a 24-hour cycle.

Some are short and some are long,
Some may inspire you,
Some may enlighten you,
Some bring up fears in you,
Some may make you sad,
Some may make you angry,
Some may make you confused,
Some may bring clarity,
Some may fill you with love,
Some may arouse you,
Some may make you laugh really hard,
Some may make you cry,
Some may make you think,
Some may fill you with peace that is beyond your own understanding.

We will pass through all these various aspects of ourselves along the way.
We will greet and embrace them all equally and we will further awaken to the wonder and magic of that which is already the case.

The intention of this journey we are taking together is to open us up as human beings to the miracle of life, which is present right now
To look at this very moment with a sense of freshness, and renewed innocence
To take in the world with a sense of wonder and utter awe,

With bewildered amazement
To quiet the mind and open the heart
To realize that you are part of a natural, creative, energetic force
that permeates the entire universe,
Including YOU
To further discover the infinite freedom of your own divine
essence and the power that lies within it.

As we continue this journey together
We will actually know much less but understand more,

Think less and live more,
Fear less and love more,
Do less and be more.

We will see this moment we are sharing together right now with
gratitude as an absolute miracle and face the fact that we really
don't know how or why it's happening. We will understand that
there are no limitations and absolutely anything is possible in the
universe, and thus in our own lives as well.

With this understanding, there is a light that begins to shine
within us and emanates out to the rest of the entire world. There
is a passion ignited in the heart and a deep sense of peace within,
like coming home for the first time.

We will call it "The Big Glow".

3- Apples

There was a very holy boy in India filled with wisdom. He had
The Big Glow shining inside him and many people would come
from miles around to be in his presence.

A well-to-do American tourist passing through the town heard
about the boy and was immediately very skeptical. He was a

very educated, sophisticated, worldly man who did not believe in God. What could a so-called "holy boy" teach him? He was determined to prove to the ignorant locals that this boy was a fraud.

One day while in the town square, he saw the boy walking followed by a crowd of devotees. He pushed and shoved his way through the crowd of locals and came up in front of the boy.

He had been waiting for this moment. He sneered at the boy and took a ripe, red apple out of his pocket. He said mockingly to the boy, "I will give you this apple if you can show me where God is?"

The boy was quiet for a moment as he stared peacefully at the man. The town's people watched. His eyes were filled with light and love. His heart was warm. Finally, he spoke in a soothing, serene voice.

"I will give you two apples if you show me where God is not."

4- The Divine Intelligence

During our journey together, the word "God" will be used from time to time. Because this word has many different meanings to many different people, I will define what this word means in the context of this book and our journey.

God here is not defined as a man or a woman in the sky, or anywhere else for that matter. It is a term used to describe the mysterious, creative force of this universe, which we are not able to comprehend with our intellects, and yet we can see reflected through all things when we are in alignment with it. This is the force that the original seers of all the world's religions attempted to point toward, through metaphor, parable, stories, verses and poem.

This force cannot seen, touched, heard, smelled, or tasted and yet when we truly come to understand it and live from it, everything we see, touch, hear, smell or taste is a reflection of it. God is everywhere and in all things.

We will come to see God in both things that are considered good
And things that are considered bad
Things that we may view as right
And also the things that we may view as wrong

5- Pronouns

Our journey is filled with many different pronouns and the reader may very well want to know whom these pronouns are referring to in this book. Pronouns such as I, you, he, she, they, we and it, as well as a few actual names thrown in for good measure.

The answer to this question is as follows:
The "I" is God, the "you" is God, the "he" is God, the "she" is God, the "they" is God, the "we" is God, the "it" is God and all the names mentioned are also God. Every single word you are reading is symbolic of the divine mystery we could call "God" taking shape through the world of form.

During this journey, we will come across a wide variety of images and forms. We will encounter many places, people and things, ideas, thoughts and feelings inside us. Embrace them all as images of the divine.

This book, like this life, is a divine play and God is playing all the roles. If you can prove me wrong, I will give you two apples!

It begins with my emancipation...

II: Before the Dawn

6- My Emancipation

From this day forward
I pronounce myself free of all border and boundaries
All restrictions
All nations
All creeds
All religions
All age groups
All ethnicities
All sects
All cults
All power
All fame
All notoriety
All churches
All denominations
All political parties
All genders
All species
All notions
All belief systems
All theories
All philosophies
All mindless blabber

In this moment
I declare myself free of all of the past
And free of all of the future

Free of all ideas
Good or bad

Free of all material cravings and greed
All time and space

All static physical forms and structures

But hereby realize the eternal flux of all physical forms and
matter
Vibrating and pulsating as myself

Everything that is built up
I tear down!

I don't even bother to tear it down
I just let it drift away
Let it evaporate and disintegrate on its own accord

Today
This very day
I pronounce myself:
FREE

Free to sing and dance
To share a laugh in the sun-filled street with perfect strangers
Free to perambulate and wander at leisure
Free to take in the round moon and swallow it whole
Free to bask in the sunshine
Free to bathe in the pure, clear-flowing waters of my soul
Free to make every sentence a poem
Every day an academy award-winning movie
Each year the best of years,
Full, rich, flowering with friends and lovers

I hereby pronounce myself
Mad
Crazy
In love with this thing called: Life
Because I now know it as my own!

I pronounce this life an art form!
And I pronounce you and I as the artists!

Go now!
Pick up your hand drum
I'll pick up my sweet guitar

And together we'll play until morning

I pronounce every atom in the universe to be a dancing butterfly
floating inside my own heart

I pronounce my new vision acute
I pronounce my senses sharp

I pronounce the earth
Cool
Smooth
Electric

I say that everything in the universe is alive
Pulsating
Moving
Interacting
Communicating

I say the universe is formless
And yet, is so great, so large,
We cannot even begin to grasp its density

I pronounce everything holy
Red rocks are holy
Young, giggling girls are holy
Old men are holy
Tiny baby does are divine
Passing, white, puffy clouds are holy
Green, grassy meadows are holy
The high, rugged mountains of Tibet and Nepal are holy

Fire burning on a cool winter's night
Young lovers loving each other in such a lovely way
Old lovers doing the same

Stray dogs barking at the stray white moon
The ant and the elephant
The slick black panther and the jackal

The white rabbit and mountain lion
Whales and sea moss
These are all cause for wonder

I pronounce everything taking place to be a miracle
I pronounce everything rising and falling moment to moment to
be of the highest wonder

I pronounce each of these words to be filled with divine magic
I pronounce every form of life to be swimming inside you
And I pronounce YOU my friend
To be the most divine wonder of all

7- The Root of the Tree

Spiritual understanding
Knowing who we really are
Is the root of the tree
If the root is healthy
The branches and leaves will follow

8- Come With Me!

Come With Me!
Come With Me!

Let's take off our masks
Let's run together
Let's race together
Let's chase down the beautiful sun
Let's make wild, passionate, spontaneous love
Without having to think twice

Let's smile together
Let's play together
Like two mystic kids running through the grass
And splashing in puddles
Let's climb trees the adults said we never could
Let's prove everybody wrong

Let's share everything
All our thoughts
All our feelings
All our fears and desires
All our money
All our food
All our clothing
All our shelter
All our bodies
And all of our hearts

Let's swim inside each other's blood
Let's explore every corner of the earth together
Let's swim across the ocean together
Climb every mountain
And slide together
Down the most beautiful tropical waterfalls
Like free-flowing driftwood

Let's have innocent minds like children

Let's forget everything we thought we knew

Let's acknowledge and embrace everything
Let's agree to always tell the truth

Let's let our long hair flow in the passing wind
And lay open, naked and free together
Underneath the warm radiant sun

Let's do things people think are crazy
Let's be fun!

Let's make this universe our home
Let's always see the divinity in each other

Let's stare in to each other's eyes for hours

Let's take time everyday to stop and smell the flowers
And laugh as hard as we can

Let's runaway together tonight!
Love will be our guide
Joy will be our home
Dance will be our movement
And laughter will be our song

We'll eat on love
We'll sleep on love
We'll live on love
We'll embody love every morning and every night

We'll teach the others how to live
We'll teach the others how to give

Love will be the fuel that carries us
And the heart will be where we fill it up!

We'll have no worries for money
Or clothes

Or shelter
Or food
Or any other material thing

All shall be provided as needed
And we will joyful discover how little is actually needed
When we carry this love in our hearts

Together we'll trust in the hands of god
We'll trust in the hands of life
We'll trust in the hands of truth
We'll trust in the hands of love

We'll be grateful for every moment we get to spend together
And consider this connection, this very moment right here a
divine miracle!

We will have no fear
We will become the universe
And the universe will become us

We'll sing and dance
Wild and naked in the meadow of colorful, blooming
wildflowers

Our hearts shall be one in love

II
Do not concern yourself with these words
For they will someday disappear

Do not concern yourself with these thoughts
For they will come and go

Do not concern yourself with this body
For it too shall have its day

But please do not forget about love
Do not forget about your spirit

Your own divine essence
For it is eternal
Do not forget who we really are
For it is timeless

Come with me today!
I will show you!
Put aside your cares and your worries

Come with me!
Let down your guard

Come forward in this very moment
Take off your mask

Join me!
Trust me!

Come with me!
Today is the first day of your life
Freedom, adventure and the greatest spiritual treasures await

Come with me!
It's never too late

Come with me today!
The journey is beginning
I see you!
I have been watching you your whole life!
Come with me!
I know you are ready!

9-
We're all angels in the making

10- Now We're Making Music!

We're making music
I hear it
Love is one sound
One voice
One word
One note
It's too full in here!
There's no room for two!
We'll have to join forces

Behind us the past is coming to an end
Before us the future is beginning
We're meeting in the middle
And sharing this moment
Our souls touch

From this moment, we carry each other forward
The music we create is up to us
I'll hold your hand if you're scared

11-
Do what feels right
Without looking for the result

12- Love Is the New Religion

On the surface of the world right now there is war and
violence and things seem dark
But calmly and quietly, at the same time, something else is
happening underground
An inner revolution is taking place and certain individuals are
being called to a higher light
It is a silent revolution
From the inside out
From the ground up

It is time for me to reveal myself
I am an embedded agent of a secret, undercover
Clandestine
Global operation
A spiritual conspiracy
We have sleeper cells in every nation on the planet

You won't see us on the T.V.
You won't read about us in the newspaper
You won't hear about us on the radio

We don't seek any glory
We don't wear any uniform
We come in all shapes and sizes
Colors and styles

Most of us work anonymously
We are quietly working behind the scenes in every country and
culture of the world
Cities big and small, mountains and valleys, in farms and
villages, tribes and remote islands

You could pass by one of us on the street and not even notice
We go undercover
We remain behind the scenes

It is of no concern to us who takes the final credit
But simply that the work gets done

Occasionally we spot each other in the street
We give a quiet nod and continue on our way so no one will
notice

During the day many of us we pretend we have normal jobs
But behind the false storefront at night is where the real
work takes place
Some call us the "Conscious Army"
We are slowly creating a new world with the power of our
minds and hearts
We follow, with passion and joy
Our orders from the Central Command
The Spiritual Intelligence Agency

We are dropping soft, secret love bombs when no one is looking
Poems
Hugs
Music
Photography
Movies
Kind words
Smiles
Meditation and prayer
Dance
Social activism
Websites
Blogs
Random acts of kindness

We each express ourselves in our own unique ways with our own
unique gifts and talents

"Be the change you want to see in the world"
That is the motto that fills our hearts
We know it is the only way real transformation takes place
We know that quietly and humbly we have the power of all the

oceans combined

Our work is slow and meticulous
Like the formation of mountains
It is not even visible at first glance
And yet with it entire tectonic plates shall be moved in the
centuries to come

Love is the new religion of the 21st century

You don't have to be a highly educated person
Or have any exceptional knowledge to understand it

It comes from the intelligence of the heart
Embedded in the timeless evolutionary pulse of all human beings

Be the change you want to see in the world
Nobody else can do it for you

We are now recruiting
Perhaps you will join us
Or already have....
All are welcome...
The door is open

13-
If you have to choose the lesser of two evils
Ask for more options

14- Hold My Hand

With every leap I take
I look across my shoulder
And you are still there smiling
Ready for the next puddle to jump and splash in

We are traveling together in to unknown regions
Of human psyche and spirit
Dimensions
And realms of being
Markers and guideposts left behind

Nothing left to grab
Or hold on to
Somewhere few human beings have yet braved to go
The flame in our hearts to guide us through the starry night

Trailblazers
On an intergalactic adventure
Venturing in to an unknown land of love
Leaving the rest of humanity behind
Blazing a trail, they will follow in the centuries to come
Hold my hand

15- Guess What?

Everybody's Right!
But some people are more right than others.

16- Lemonade

In the time before we were born
We are all there picking lemons
At birth, we made a conscious decision to turn them in to
lemonade
It's starting to taste really good!
You take a sip out of my glass
And I will take a sip out of yours

17-

Live as if you're already dead
Deep peace
Nothing to fear

18- Colors of the Self

My white is pure and innocent
Like winter snowflakes gently floating toward the horizon

My gray is subdued and mellow
Like sea lions sleeping in the morning
Along the foggy California coast line

My purple is majestic and grand
Like the kings' finest robes

My pinks are feminine, soft and giggly
Like bubble gum and blooming carnations

My red is filled with love, passion and eros
Like the red swollen lips of beautiful, sexy woman
Ready to be kissed

My blue is tranquil and easy
Like the clear, Sunday afternoon sky in early September
Like a still and tranquil mountaintop lake
Filled with the purest, clearest, mountain water

My yellow is cheerful and silly
Like daffodils and bumblebees in the Spring

My orange is hot, juicy and tropical
Like old grapefruits baking in the radiant, late afternoon sun

My green is comfortable and grounding
Like lazily, laying in the Spring grass in the warm, fresh
afternoon
Engrossed in a favorite novel

My browns are fertile and deeply rooted
Like thick, ancient tree trunks
Like the deep, rich soil from which we spring

My black is strong and full of mystery
Like the endless night sky above the open prairie

I embrace all the colors inside me
Open up my book
And see my rainbow

19-
The man who is not ready to die for love
Is not ready to live for it

20- YOU

I met you
In the future
You are an incredible person!

III: SUNRISE

21-Like Rain

Poetry falls
Like rain

I'm outside now
Getting wet

Here comes the lightning!
Let's see if I can put it in a bottle!

22-

Laugh with the laughter of little children and great sages

23- Poem of Life

This poetry, these words, insights and inspirations have begun
falling from the sky and into my lap recently in
endless variety

I know not from where

Like the sweetest cherries from the most ancient tree...
Let's gather them in to a small clay-fired bowl
And eat them in the open meadow underneath the evening
stars

I suddenly see poems everywhere
The sky
The open fields
The shape of a dolphin
The taste of a grape

I am transcribing it as quickly as I can
Whenever I can

Breathing in the sweet, dense, mystery of life
And breathing out the poems from which they came

I am writing them in the stars
Casting them in rivers
Throwing them in lakes
Dancing with them in the evening
Sleeping inside them in the afternoon
And placing them deep in the hearts of my fellow human beings
When we look closer
There is a deeper flow and melody to the day
The universe is singing a song
Life itself becomes the grandest poem
I see your life as a part of that poem

24-
There is nothing wrong with you
And yet you have unlimited potential inside you.

25- Together

Together we dream so deeply we see it in front of us
everywhere we look
We are living in a world of dreams
I believe in my imagination with all my heart
I believe in your imagination as well
I believe our dreams are connected

26-
There is not one person in the world more beautiful than the
person reading this right now

27-
See the beauty in others
Even if they are not currently behaving in a way you would
prefer

Believe in them
Don't give up

Treat people the way you would like them to be
And they may indeed become that one day

28-
When I look back on my life, I realize that my life is a dream and
I played all the characters

29- My Presentation

It's brand new!
Currently being unveiled!

In this day!
In this very hour!!
I announce
The moment called "Now"!!

30-
To see the world
Is to see your own self staring back at you
How do you look?

31- About the American Heart Land

The mass media have divided the American people up into "Red" and "Blue" and invested a lot of energy to exacerbate tensions between us. This is an effort to diffuse some of that tension and begin to move in a productive way to begin to create the world we all would like to see. To encourage us to see past preconceived labels and truly listen to what those who are different than us have to share. America is full of many different subcultures. This is a reminder to recognize the humanity and perhaps even the divinity within us all.

I took the train this past weekend from Colorado to Pennsylvania, which was an exhausting, yet quite amazing experience. On the train were Americans from all walks of life, both "Red" and "Blue". We were stuck together on the train for two days.

Something quite amazing was happening. For two days, we shared handshakes, hugs, good wishes, laughs, music, stories, advice, food, money. We didn't care what we were labeled. It never came up.

There was great diversity among us, but what we felt on a deeper level was the common humanity that binds us at the level of the heart...

So to you my reader, whether we're traveling through the East, the West, the Deep South, or Middle America,
May we always be in the Heart Land.

The following was written on that train ride rolling through Nebraska with the first hints of daylight and is dedicated to our brothers and sisters who are labeled Red, Conservative, Traditional...
I can still see the divinity within you and the beautiful prairie land you walk upon. This one's for you...

32- Sunrise over Nebraska

Sunrise over Nebraska
The countryside slowly waking up

In the long open fields of corn and barley
Ducks playing in the still sunlit ponds
From last night's replenishing rain
The cows and pigs stretching their legs and basking in the
morning light
As the roosters noisily greet the new day
As if the sun could hear them
The horses are strong and handsome in their stable
Old blue pick-up trucks drive down quaint old farm roads,
kicking out black smoke from their tail pipes

The men are simple, grounded, sturdy, strong, and robust
They grab another bag of feed from the truck in the morning light

The women are stronger and clear-eyed
Trying to raise their children the right way, following what the
bible teaches

Life here is simple
Just like the previous generation

Things move at a slower pace
The values are strong

In the morning, it's church
In the afternoon, it's football

Long, wide, endless horizons
In every direction

Sunrise over Nebraska
The grass a vibrant green

A prayer of gratitude for this fertile land
The endless horizon
The gentle sun this morning that warms the hearts of every soul it touches

Before enlightenment
Harvest the field
And say your prayers before bed

After enlightenment
Harvest the field
And say your prayers before bed

33- An Insight about Kisses

The Loudest Kisses Are The Ones On Your Ears.

34- The Game of Man and Woman

Let's play a game!

You be the woman
And I'll be the man

You be soft
And I'll be hard

You be small
And I'll be big

You be weak
And I'll be strong

You have curves
I'll have sharp angles

You be wet
And I'll be dry

You be the moon
I'll be the sun

You be the Earth
And I'll be the sky

You be the yin
And I'll be the yang

You be this side of the universe
And I'll be the other

You be receptive
And I'll be giving

You be open

And I'll be assertive

You provide the nest
And I'll bring home the treasures

You be nurturing
And I'll be stern

You give me comfort
And I'll give you adventure

You be the mother
And I'll be the father

You be the daughter
And I'll be the son

You be the sister
And I'll be the brother

You be the Aunt
And I'll be the Uncle

You be the Grandma
And I'll be the Grandpa

You be the waitress
And I'll be the waiter

You be the Goddess
And I'll be the God

You be Spring
And I'll be Autumn

You tend to birth
And I'll tend to death

You be the sea

And I'll be the river

You be the valley
And I'll be the mountain

You be being
And I'll be form

You be the feminine
And I'll be the masculine
And together we dance
You be the feminine
And I'll be the masculine
And together like two great artists
We create the whole universe

You be the feminine
And I'll be the masculine
And together like two great artists
We create a beautiful family

You be the feminine
And I'll be the masculine
And together we create community

You be the feminine
And I'll be the masculine
And together we create erotic union

You be the feminine
And I'll be the masculine
And together we make love

Let me move further inside you
As you get to know me better and trust me

Remember, it's just a game!

35-
See the mystery in your partner
With each moment

36- You Are

You are an Incredible Divine Being...
Perfect in every way just as you are...

Your presence here on this planet has benefitted more beings than
you realize...
And you're just getting started!

Just wanted to remind you...

37- Smart Class

The teacher asked his class, "What's the difference between
ignorance and apathy?"
They responded. "We don't know and we don't care."

38- The Universe Is a Mirror

I woke in the morning
I heard the robins and the doves singing for breakfast
I saw the sun creeping over the hill
Causing the darkness to disappear
And bringing long shadows to the morning trees
Filled with birds and ripe fruit
The grass and flowers outside were moist and filled with dew
There is a stillness this morning
A deep quiet that cannot be put in words

Everything is fresh
New
Reborn

This earth
And the entire universe
Is a mirror

It's wonderful this morning
To see my reflection
Everywhere I look

39-
Let Love Be Your Guide
And It Will Be a Much Smoother Ride

40-
The heart is the most intelligent organ in the body
It has a computing ability that is more precise, direct and accurate
than anything within the limits of rational thought

41-
In this moment, we will never find what we are looking for
But if we stop looking
We may discover something even better

42- Acrobat Dawn

Morning time
I rose up
Jumped out of bed
Hit the shades
And saw the acrobat dawn

Why an Acrobat Dawn?
Because when I first took in the beauty of the sunrise
My heart did flips!

43- Love

If you do something without wanting anything in return
You have everything you want!

44- The Miracle of This Moment

No two things are alike
Or ever will be
No two moments are alike
Or ever will be
Therefore this moment right now
Is something you have never experienced
Your entire life
And never will again

If you're not paying attention
You will take it for granted
Please don't

45-

This world is like a bridge
Pass over it
But don't build a house upon it

46- A New Song

Jasmine growing underneath the steps
At daybreak
In the morning light
In the sunshine
With a soft breeze blowing through the wisdom of the ancient
trees

The dance of morning magic brings seductive memories to mind
And visions of dazzling sunrises yet to arise

I hear the first melody of the morning songbird
There is a new song rising in her soul

47-

All suffering is based in ignorance of one's true nature

48- What Do You want?

You want to be free?
Take your time
Go leisurely and easily

Do things slow
And never do more than what needs to be done

But what needs to be done
Do that with excellence

Enjoy every moment
Taste every sunrise

49-

Life is a spontaneous poem

50- Life Is The Teacher!

Did you forget why you're here?

Life is the teacher and life is the school. The proper lessons are in front of us in each moment. The challenges we may be facing right now in our lives are exactly the ones we are supposed to be facing in exactly this moment to learn the exact lessons we are supposed to be learning. Everything is perfectly designed for us to grow and evolve in our consciousness, to deepen us, provide us with self-awareness and wisdom, and bring us further in to the light, the big glow!

Therefore instead of diverting energy with complaints and victimization, let us channel and focus our energy toward gratefully embracing and trusting in each moment and challenge in our lives as an opportunity to continually grow and learn.

Glad to provide the reminder.

51-
The key in professional life is not to be rich or famous but to be great

52- Take Off

Longing for the unified heart
The infinite dream

Footprints in the clouds
Jumping off into heaven

53- In the Light

In the light that brings me closer
No wants
No needs
No desires
Just surrender

54- His Painting for Her

He is going to paint a picture of her and start with her heart
Painting it red and big with shining, golden rays radiating out in
all directions
The warm love emanating from it to all who enter her presence

He paints her eyes
Those beautiful, green eyes are almost dangerous
Radiant! Glowing!
Ferocious like a tiger
With a sense of magic and play
Fun
Deep awareness
And presence
Bordering on sheer madness

When those eyes lock with the love-force, intensity and zest of
his own eyes, an incredible electrical, chemical energy fills the
space between them
And, in fact, fills the entire room

This energy has no limits!
It can turn sinners into saints
Water in to wine
A caterpillar in to a butterfly
And free the slaves when they are ready
It could be tapped by NASA to send rockets to the moon!
Or even to start eyeball power plants (better than nuclear or fossil
fuel)!

58

He paints the hair flowing, dark and long
Wild and free like her spirit
Unbound
Like the beautiful mane of a wild horse
Loose and free in the open prairie

Then perhaps her skin, soft and smooth
Copper and warm
The thin covering for her bright, shining soul

He wants to paint her smiling
Her pure, innocent smile
Makes him smile himself

He paints many colorful waves and patterns around her forehead
to symbolize the workings of her mind
Contemplative
Thoughtful
Bright
Articulate

He adds many different colors in and around the painting to
symbolize the complexity of her emotions and her personality
Her hopes
Her dreams
And her fears

He paints her amidst a field of wildflowers
That is the place that fits her best
On a clean, fresh, April morning
With the big, sun slowly rising over the Eastern horizon
And long shadows slowly receding from the warming, green
Spring grass

For companionship, he paints her hundreds of butterflies and
bumblebees
To talk to
Laugh with
Dance with

Make love to
Cry to

And a beautiful forest to surround it
With big, beautiful, voluptuous dark, juicy berries

Vibrant fruits and vegetables everywhere
And a diversity of friendly, peaceful animals
Who enjoy being petted
And sharing with her in the beauty of her day

He will paint a big, magical, mystical, mountain range as a
backdrop
So that she can always contemplate, ponder and meditate upon
the wonder of its every ridge and fold

And how about painting a hint of the ocean in the distance
For long moonlight swims with friendly dolphins

Together they will paint with magical colors
They will paint the world they want to create
Step inside it
Open their eyes
Dance to the magical, musical rhythms of Nature
And disappear forever and ever

55-
You're Going To Die Soon! Do it now!

56- The Present

This moment is completely New.
This moment is a Gift we are given.
That is why in the English language it's called the Present.
May we untie the bow and see what lies inside.

57-
Mystery is at the root of all we see
So take in the world with selfless wonder

58-
The degree to which you show your ignorance is the degree to
which you find your truth

59- Music

Music
So beautiful when it touches your soul
So sweet when it enters your ears
And comes out through your tappin' feet
I prefer it loud
Let it play
Music
Let my body sway

Do you know that everything is music?
The way the elderly woman breathes

The way the clouds slowly drift across the sky on their way
towards Africa
A place you and I may never go
But which the clouds sing to us about

The way the water splish-splashes along the bank of the creek
On its way to wider water

Brass horns
And drums of all sizes
That make you bob your head with approval

Guitars and Sitars
And big stand-up basses

My voice
And your voice
The sound of children
And gospel choirs

The rhythmic taps on the keyboards of the laptops in the coffee
shop

The thumpin' hip-hop beat of the city
Sweet banjo playin' chords from the mountains of Kentucky

Do you know that everything is music?

The sun rising through the mist
On your lips a gentle kiss
The hum-hum of the souped-up Chevy
Eggs frying on the stove
Potatoes baking in the oven

The sound of the brush as it runs through your hair
The song of the drifter who doesn't have a care

The man talking on his cell phone about things he could really
wait to talk about until he gets home

The way the wind whistles through the leaves
A different vibration and tone for each

Life is playing a melody
All throughout the day

A universal chorus
And ongoing symphony

"Universe" means "one song"
Are you listening?

60-
If you could understand God
It wouldn't be God!

IV: Morning

61-The Awakening

My eyes opened this morning
And I was given a gift
A new day filled with untold adventures

62-

Surprise!!!
Life is filled with them!

63- The Greatest Brian Piergrossi

I remember it well
The astounding realization
Early morning
Driving in the car
When suddenly it dawned on me

I am the greatest Brian Piergrossi that ever lived!!

64-

My career is following the dictates of my heart
What's yours?

65- The Oatmeal's Hot

Early morning
Long shadows
Across green grass
Come inside!
Don't wait!
The oatmeal's hot!
Just add honey!

66-
Surrender is an openness to reality

67- Taking a Stand

Don't let anyone push you around today.
Don't do what you're told unless you also feel its right.
Don't except half-truths from anyone.
Don't accept that someone is more knowledgeable than you
unless they prove it to be so.
Do not think that someone is worthy of your admiration just
because they have money and fancy material gadgets. In most
cases, they are not.

Listen to your heart.
Do what it tells you do to and who cares if it's possible or not.
You may go hungry for a little while but not forever.
You may lose your job but you probably didn't like it anyway.
You may be ridiculed but probably only by people who are
themselves ridiculous.
You may lose friends but you will gain others.
If someone wants to unload their baggage on you tell them you
are not a table.
Stand up! You've been sitting down too long.
Take a stand for something and others will follow.

68-
For winners
Losing inspires them tremendously

69- Extraordinarily Ordinary

Ordinary day
Hop inside the car
Turn the key
Turn on the radio
Put the car in reverse
Then put it in drive
Sun rising up over the mountains
Birds chatting about their breakfast
A strange stillness in the air

Suddenly it occurred to me:
I feel good
But I don't know the reason

70-
What stands in the Way
IS the Way

71- Hillbilly Psalms

I grew out of the soil of the rolling hills of Pennsylvania
Covered with snow in the Winter
Flowers in the Spring
Deep greens in the Summer
And falling leaves in the Autumn

But tonight I want to sing a song about the Southland
I wanna whistle some Dixie
Because I saw it once in a Yankee dream
And today the dream was realized

As the morning sun rises up to greet us from behind
We're cruisin' through the Carolina mountains at breakneck
speed
Shirts off
Shoes off
Windows down
My son suddenly shouts from the back with inspiration
"Dad, I wannna hear some Cowboy music!"
And I say, "Y'all wanna hear some cowboy music?"
And I flip the dial to something about "a redneck woman"

Driving deeper in through the heart of the Southern
Appalachians now
Wildflowers surrounding us on all sides
I feel the Bluegrass music filling my heart
Hear the Honky Tonk seeping into my soul
And over the ridge lies the Land of the Delta Blues

I can hear the sweet fiddle, and the banjo,
The voices gathered around a single microphone singing in sweet
harmony
Stand-up basses and slide-guitars

In the morning as the sun rises up like a fire
I'll pass on the chitlins, but please pass the grits!
In the afternoon, I see the purty gals smilin' and strolling through

the sunshine in their beautiful Summer dresses and cowgirl boots
I hope they don't mind if I catch another glance
If I had a hat, I'd tip it in their direction

There's no need to rush here
This aint like the big city where everyone is chasing the future
Right now is good enough for us

Whatever we don't get done today
We'll take care of it tomorrow

I see the friendly folks along the countryside waving to me as we drive by
I believe that's called Southern Hospitality

At night the folks and I converse under the moon and around the fire
We sing old-time songs about hobo life and hoppin' trains
As we pass around the communal guitar

I bid everyone good night and the boy and I head back through the night, which is as quiet and still as a photograph, yet somehow vibrant and alive

Inside my tent, I lay my head back and peacefully fall asleep to a quiet symphony of crickets and bullfrogs

I dream of the trees around me
They tell me their stories
And sing me their songs

I'm falling in love with these hills
I guess that makes me a hillbilly

72-

"I fell awake." -Jillian, 4 years old, after a long sleep

73- It's Good to Be Selfish!

There are different levels of happiness and fulfillment in this life.
The highest level of fulfillment and happiness comes when one
feels connected, a part of this universe, this earth, and its people.
When one knows there is no illusionary separation between
oneself and the outside world...
What once felt to be outside shifts and the whole world now feels
as if it's part of your inside
Part of your very own body!

Now what one does
One does with great energy and vitality
With the benefit of all beings in mind
With compassion
For the new larger Self
And for the highest Love

When there is no sense of separation
There is no fear
And there is only love
One radiates light
And there is a natural desire to nurture and care for this world

The highest fulfillment comes in giving all you have to give to
this world in every moment and in each movement

This is the energy called Love
And when one is lost in love,
One completely forgets oneself
Losing all sense of self-consciousness and narcissism
Completely lost in the moment
And therein lies the greatest freedom
And the highest fulfillment.

It's good to be selfish! It's good to want to feel happy and
fulfilled! But be selfish in an intelligent way that really works!
That will really bring the purest and deepest fulfillment to
yourself and others without negative repercussions.
It's a win-win proposition.

74- Fear and Love

There are two basic energies in the universe
Fear and Love
Which do you want to be in?
It's your choice.
Please choose now.

75-

Today is like a diamond
It's shining for you!

76- Why I Am a Hypocrite

In the future
I would like to find someone
Who doesn't think about the future so much

77- Truckin'

Renewed and rejuvenated
After a good night's sleep
French fries and cold, dark beer

I am like a fireball
Rolling through the lights of an interstate dream

Headlights flashing
Sirens roaring
Horn honking
Music blasting

Blood, sweat and tears
On eighteen wheels
A fire-breathing cannonball of rocket fuel
Jet-like thunder

Hear me rumble
As I roar down the freeway in a blanket of smoke
Feel my engine
Hear the hum of the motor
As I slam my foot on the gas
See the light turn green
I'm a beautiful stallion
White lightening in the sky
Moving through life at breakneck speed
The engine's hot
The dash is electric
Hear the gears shift
Racing down the bend

I'm truckin'

Next stop
Your house

78-
Do you really want change?
If so
It is a much better approach to foster the positive
Than attack the negative

79-
It's good to say, "I don't know." It opens you up to this moment.

80- God's Pond

Release the mind of all its attachments
Let it float free and untainted

Like the clear reflection
Of your own beautiful face
In God's Pond of Love

81-
Because he was unable to accept his life spontaneously
He made it into a problem

82- Catch the Light

Catch the light!
Feel the light!
Be filled with the light
Consumed by it

Let it eat you like a sandwich
Let it work you into a frenzy
And drop you off into a town you've never before been
Like a tornado!

Let it envelope you like hot fire
And send you into the blissful ashes
Of a place beyond limits and categories

Postage paid

83-
What we seek
 Seeks us

84- First Taste

First taste
Life springs forward
From the realm of infinite possibility
The vast sea of the unknown

From the empty void
Bursting with creation
Like Cherry Burst
Exploding on all conceivable horizons
So juicy
So fresh

Ready to taste
The moment your mouth begins to salivate
Take a bite
And chew slowly

85-
To be fully aware of death
Is to be fully aware of life

86- New Morning

I woke up to a bright sunny morning
Life was fresh
And I realized I can do
And be
And feel
Anything that I want
Love is life
And life is love
Remember this
And good things will come
Like the shining sun
As it arises in the morning

When the sky was blue
And soft wind blew
Past my lips
And through my nose
I breathed it out fully
And I smiled
And thanked the ONE

The birds were singing
The grass was green
The flowers were blooming
By the crystal clear creek
That's when I knew I was alive

Don't let life get you down too long
And if it does
Just think of these words
Yesterday has nothing to do with today

When the sun sat low
And the crickets sung out
And a squirrel strolled by
With a nut in his mouth
That's when I knew I'd be alright

87-

Mommy: Little Johnny, what to do you want to be when you
grow up... a doctor... or a lawyer?
Little Johnny: A Saint.

88- All Natural

This morning the hills are filled with magic
And moist with dew

The trees standing tall and stoic
The sky the deepest of blues

A few soft pillowy clouds
Slow dance across the horizon

A slight breeze is felt
To remind me I'm alive

The birds are singing
Not to reach any goal
But for the joy of singing

A deer suddenly dashes across the meadow
With spell-binding grace

I take an indrawn breath
The air is clean, fresh, exuberant

Life is present
Life is here
Life is right now
Life is beautiful

And thus, the question arises
Where does nature stop and I begin?
Today I can't find the boundary

89-
Everything is in the nature of the miraculous

90- Picking Sweet Cherries

In this quiet Sunday morning
Let this connection be our church
Let these words be our dance
Let their rhythm be our love
And their light shine our way

As we walk this path
And dance this dance
And play our roles in this most powerful play
May we remind each other who we really are

Now
And always
There is only this moment
And it is here we lie together
Smelling the flowers
And picking sweet cherries!

91-
This morning I looked into the mirror and I saw God

92- The Sweet Flower

Crisp, fall, fresh, sea breeze, Western Coast, America air floating
through these nostrils
Fresh, oxygen-rich and oak-scented
Drifting across the vast blue Pacific from mysterious places like
mystic China and the zendos of Japan

Wondrous places where young Buddhas eat hot soup and wake
up at dawn
Observing the way the sunshine hits a lovely tree on a Saturday
morning
The way its shadow gently falls across its neighbor, the still blue
lake
And they softly smile with that feeling of completeness

Life is just a sweet flower
Take a whiff some time

93-
Every day is a subtle flower
Tend to it like a gardener

94- Lunch Date

Beyond ideas about both the past and the future
There is a place too amazing to be put in words
Let's meet there today for lunch
And have a feast of gigantic proportions!

95-
God is growing older and wiser too

96- On the Set

Your life is a movie
And you are the star!
Action!!

97- Some Things Are Beautiful

Some things are beautiful
Like the huge, red sun
Amidst the clear, blue sky
On an August, Summer morning

Warm.
Hot
Loving

Touching down its rays equally on every form of life
A gentle wind blowing through the swaying green trees

The afternoon grows quiet and tender
And the day flows on with equanimity and grace like a soft poem

Whatever work needs to be done
We'll take care of it tomorrow

98-
Do you think God believes in God?

99- Forest Fire

Passion can be contagious
When you first catch it
On a dew drop morning
Or walking amidst the ancient twilight
Quietly gazing up at the crystal clear, effervescent, midnight sky
Or taking in a breath of cool, crisp invigorating, fresh air

Listening to majestic music that makes your heart sprout out
fireworks of deep color and vibrancy

Seeing a young man in the street
And knowing he's just like you

Seeing an old bum smiling on the corner
And knowing he's more free than you are

Watching a white moth gently floating across the bushes
Or watching the hot, pinkish-red sun melt in to the green hills
like strawberry ice cream
And knowing it will be back tomorrow

Knowing if you won a million dollars you'd throw it in the street

Seeing a beautiful woman
And knowing there's no need to possess her in any way

Listening to my heart beat in perfect rhythm
Watching the air move in and out of my lungs
Watching my digestive system working its wonders
Dumping the excess out the back end
Which in time will fertilize fruits and berries
And grow trees which I will climb up in to
Sit inside
And read poetry filled with Spiritual Vitamins
As the late afternoon sun slides down my back
Through the strong, ancient branches

Have you ever met a happy man?
Come and shake my hand
I'm in the forest
And it's starting to catch fire

100-
Which Direction To Go?
Nowhere But Up...........!

101- Your Computer

There is no inherent, fixed reality to the mind
Like a computer
You can program it any way you choose

That's the good news!
What programs are YOU running?

102-
All suffering is the space between what you think should be and
what is

103- Different Kinds of Soulmates

Who is the person who challenges you the most in your life?
They are one of your greatest soulmates
They provide the greatest opportunity for learning and growth
Be grateful for the challenges they present to you
You will be better because of it

104-
The Best Is Always Yet To Come

105- Shadow Boxing

What you are drawn to or despise in others
Are often just the qualities of your own shadow
You would like more of or less of in yourself

106-
Make every day your prayer

107- Mystery

There is only one thing and that is the Mystery
In the beginning, there is the mystery
In the middle, there is the mystery
In the end, the exact same mystery

108-
If this moment is golden, why do you need a next one?

109- To Be a Life Artist

To be an artist
Is to live fully
Directly
Vitally
Without regard to merit or reward
But to flow
Endlessly
Rocking the boat
Whichever way feels right

Following the inner urge to express any masterpiece of the
moment
No matter how little or small
And no one can tell you the price of its worth
Except your own inner organs

The inner urge to create
And procreate
And Live
Love
Learn

Feel it in your fingers and toes
Bouncing
Pulsing
Vibrating
Feel it in your sexual organs
Your heart
Your liver
Your spleen

Feel it throughout your day
The rollercoaster
The up and downs

Feel it in the center of town
In the boondocks of Idaho

Or the heart of Mexico
Feel it along the Pacific Ocean
So vast and blue
Feel it in the humming buzz of the concrete streets
Feel it with your bare feet deep in the fertile, muddy earth

Tune in!
Feel it inside you
Loud and Clear
The same place it's always been!

110-
When they're being bad
Hit 'em with poetry!

111-
The first step
Is the last step
Once you've gone all the way
You realize you are back in the exact same place you started
Just seeing it from an entirely different perspective

112-
There are no wholes and no parts at any point in the universe.
There are only whole parts.

113-
Let us take care of each other
Wc're all we have

114-

The world is waiting for you
And the world is waiting for me
Let's not let them wait any longer
Let's step into the light

115-

The Past and the Future
Are a complete illusion

116- The Smell of the Lilacs

The world shimmers in infinite sunlight
Treetops dance to the call of the wind's whisper

Children play and laugh
In the land where they let the children play and laugh

Oh Lord, why have you blessed us this way?
Why have you cherished us this way?
This rooftop covers my vacant mind
A few white clouds streak across the sky
Blue like a young boy's crib

I can now hear the titter-tatter of the wind
As it rustles through the leaves
A background song
To the visual dance

A red-breasted robin flies across my view
Strong and Free
Now he sits perched in the tree above me
With several of his friends
And together they sing a song taught by their elders
The same song their family has sung for generations

I smell the scent of the lilacs in through my open window
The only thing I recall in my life that ever smelled so good
Is Mommy's chocolate chip cookies
Fresh and piping hot out of the oven
On a cold December, Saturday afternoon
When I was a boy in that blue crib
Tucked in the valley
Of the rolling green hills of Pennsylvania

Or that first smell of the ocean
After a long period of absence from it
That smell in which you know that everything is alive
And connected to the vast body of water that stretches out in
front of you
Which is the largest living organism in the world
And you're blessed to have a swim
You can even smell the pink moon rising above it in the evening
In all cases
It's the smell of freedom
The smell of falling deeply in love with this moment
So in love, one becomes lost in the smell itself
And life is a gift
Just as it IS!

It's in these cases
That past and future fall away

It's in these cases
That the divine mystery arises

It's in these cases
That I know
That I really don't know

117-
Fixed Ideas Are A False Form Of Protection

118- Life

Life
A series of images
Appearing and disappearing
What do yours look like?

119- The Enlightened Grasshopper

Someone seeking enlightenment is like a grasshopper trying to understand what it is like to be a grasshopper.

120- Woman Come Forth

Woman
The long day is over
Take off your pants and put on a skirt

Woman come forth
Your soft touch can heal me
Your soft words sooth me
You bring music to my heart

So gentle
Natural
Graceful

So mysterious
And mystical

With you, I feel complete
With you, I feel whole
In your loving eyes I feel at home
As a child
I could lay forever with my head on your soft, round breasts,
underneath your long, soft hair
As a man, I can do the same
Every curve of your body speaks of beauty
Every inch has divine stories to tell
When you smile
God is present
When you sleep
I feel the serenity of your soul
When you laugh
I feel happy
When you cry
I lend you my shoulder

Woman
So natural
So gentle
So graceful

Woman
Your heart can save the world
Woman come forth
We need your essence

121-
ENJOY YOUR KARMA !

122- The Humorous Search

I am searching for the person who isn't searching for anything.
Would you mind
Helping me search for them?

123- Meaning in Life

Has anyone ever asked you "What is the meaning of life?"
Have you ever asked yourself that question?
What a terrible question!

The meaning of life is to live!
There is no meaning of life
There is meaning IN life
In this very moment

The meaning of breathing is to breathe
The meaning of running is to run
The meaning of eating is to eat

Not to achieve any goal
Not to receive any accolades or praise

When the light turns red, you stop
When the light turns green, you go

A young man once walked 500 miles to see a revered spiritual
sage
When he finally arrived, he saw the revered sage sitting in his
front yard
He walked up to him and nervously said,
"Sir, I have just walked 500 miles to see you and to ask you this
most important question: How do I find Enlightenment?"
The sage looked at him
"Have you eaten breakfast?"
"Yes" The man replied
"Wash you bowl" The sage said
The young man instantly became enlightened.

There once was a poetry contest in the great state of Alaska
All contestants were asked to write a poem about Mt. McKinley
All kind of flowery language was used
A young man entered the contest and recited the following three
lines:

Mt. McKinley
Mt. McKinley
Ohhhhhhhhhh Mt. McKinley!

He won first prize and walked out

When someone writes a poem
Don't ask them to explain it
When someone breaks out in song
Don't ask them why
When a baby cries
He has no ulterior motives
When it rains
It's not to make your garden grow

Rumi said, the miracle of Jesus was in the way he lived his life
Not in what he said or did about the future.
He said forget about the future!
He'd worship somebody who could do THAT!

The meaning of life is to live
To be fully engaged
To be fully alive
To fully participate

Get up off the sidelines!
Get on the field and get dirty!

If you're angry
Be so angry you could kill

If you're horny
Be so horny you want to hump everything that moves

If you're sad
Be so sad you could fill a river with your tears

If you're afraid

Be completely and utterly terrified

If you're lost
Be utterly, mystically bewildered

If you're joyful
Be so joyful you could jump over the moon
And swim through the stars

If you're happy
And you know it
Clap your hands!
Don't carry anything!
Travel through the day naked
Open and exposed
And damn the consequences!

Drop flowers wherever you go

Die completely to this moment
And be completely born again in the next

Life is not a series of events
It's not an uphill battle

It's an explosion
Happening right here and now!
An intergalactic, cosmic orgasm!

Not when you retire
Not after the kids are grown
Not when the pension kicks in
Not next year
Not next month
Not next week
Not tomorrow
Not in a few hours
Not in a few moments
Right now!

Meaning
Purpose
And Inspiration
Here is where it's at!

124-
Every moment is an orgasm!

125- Without a Why

The morning flower is without a why
It blooms because it blooms

126- Soft Love Drops

It's fun to have so many different ways to sprinkle soft, love
drops on you
You are starting to get wet
Don't reach for an umbrella

127-

Without Imagination, of what importance is knowledge?

128- Presence

Our degree of presence
And attention
To this moment
Creates both
Our future
And our past
In this moment
May we create a thrilling future
And a rich and storied past

129- Many Paths

There are many paths to God.
Choose one...!

130- Growing Wings

I look around me
Day in and day out
I see the walking zombies
Waiting to pick up their paychecks on Friday
And fall face first into their open caskets

I look around and I want to cry out
I want to scream from the bottom of my lungs
"Wake up and touch life!
It's right in front of you!"

I want to shout it from the highest mountaintop
Let my words fall across their faces like a fresh spring rain
A rainbow of life

There's an energy
A magic to it
When it comes upon you with all its force

Feel it in your toes as you bounce across the street
Feel it in your legs as you bounce across the meadow
Feel it in your feet as you kick away the past
Feel the vibrancy of it in your genitals
Your sexual organs
Feel the fresh air move through your lungs as you take an
indrawn breath
Let your ears dance to the sounds all around them

Feel it in your heart as it welcomes every experience

Swallow Everything!
Both bitter and sweet

Feel it in your hair as the wind blows through it
Sing every song you know

Turn the day into a melody

And damn the consequences

Throw away your money
Put down your precious books
Tell a joke and laugh like hell
Kick away your crutches
And see if you can walk

Wake up and touch life!
Even if it's just for a moment
It will carry you for days

Tell the preacher to come back next Sunday
Tell the Rabbi you have no time for commandments

Life is vital!

Tell your enemies you have no time to be angry at them
Tell your friends they can come if they wish

In the sky
I see a beautiful bird

Look Closely!
You're growing wings
And it's time to take flight

131-
What I finally realized is
Anything is possible
In any moment
Nothing is assured
Not even dying

132- Enlightenment

Enlightenment:
It's not what you think it is!

133- A Cheesy Life

The trouble with the rat race
Is that even when
You finally get the cheese
You're still a rat!

134-
Relax
Open up
To the miracle of life

135- Just Like Poetry

Life is beautiful
When it shines down
Like clear blue sky
On an August Summer morning
Warm, hot, loving
The sun, touching down its rays
Equally, on every form of life
A gentle wind at your back
And the day flows
With equanimity and grace
Like Poetry

136-
Time keeps on moving
But the love that moves
From heart to heart
Is timeless

V: Afternoon

137- 12 O'clock Noon

It's morning
But it's 12 o'clock noon

The cold sun is shining
In a clear blue sky

Thin white snow
Covers this world like icing

A few leaves remain
Hanging frightfully to their tree
Wondering when it will be their turn to jump

It's morning
But it's 12 o'clock noon

138-
Expectation Is Limitation

139- Like Wild Coyotes

High noon in the Northern meadow
The red sun is perched deep inside a hazy sky
Like a falcon ready to spread its wings

After a long Winter
The air has become thick and humid
As if Mother Nature were coming closer to us again with all her
warmth
Softly whispering in our ears with her hot moist air
Reminding us once again that we are loved and not forgotten

The trees are dressed in a million blooming flowers
Vibrant pinks and violets

Most human beings are too busy trying to make money on a
weekday afternoon
So, I take in the beauty and fragrance of the flowers with
the geese and the ducks
They already have all the money they need!

Looking down into the shimmering creek below
I see a reflection of a huge oak tree
Big, strong branches hundreds of years in the making

I want to climb up inside those branches
Dream of things not yet possible and imagine them so

The afternoon air has struck a match
There is a fire inside my heart

Tonight let's roast marshmallows
And howl at the moon like wild coyotes

140-
Your Biography
Does Not Determine Your Future!

141- Hunger

My hunger is insatiable
Unbearable
Uncontrollable

I wish to grab life by its mystical pulse
To devour the tree of life
Eat it from the roots up
To its thick trunk of vital life force

Eat all its juicy branches and twigs
Its leaves and berries
I want to devour the entire tree of life
In one huge gulp

And feel it fully in this moment!

Fill my belly up
And burp with pleasure

Life is one big timeless explosion
And I'm on the bomb squad!

The Big Bang is happening
What's for dessert?

142-
Laughter is God
Tickling your ribs

143- Beyond Definition

You are not your name
Your car
Your house
Your spouse
Your money
Your job
Your past
Or your future
You are this moment

144-

We're creating the human experience because we love stories and games

145- The Da Da Poem

A Da- Da- Da- Da- Da- Da
Life Goes on

Good times
Well- Da- Da- Da- Da- Da- Da
Life Goes on

Bad times
Yes- Da- Da- Da- Da- Da- Da
Life Goes on

146-

Keep other people's hands off your brain

147- Love Is Not a Thing

Excessive thinking about things generates fear
The more things you think you've gained and now own
The more you think you must protect those things
For fear of losing those things
The more you are living your life for things
The more you are living your life in fear
And not for love
Love is not fear
Love is something no one can ever take from you
Love is not something you can gain or lose
Love is the most powerful force in the universe
Love is not a thing

148-

It's not important that people love you
It's only important that you love them

149-

All problems
Are really just divine challenges
Great opportunities for spiritual growth

150-

Who were you before you knew anything?

151- Fall from Grace

Sometimes I sit and take in the children
I see how they smile
With spontaneity and innocence
Like lightning in the Summer sky

I see the bounce in their step
I see the music in their stride
Free as birds
And sweet like candy
God is a man in the clouds
And life is dandy

Then what happens?

152-
Today I am madly in love with everyone!

153-
Let the children play
Whatever game they choose
As long as it's creative

154-
Deal with the challenges in your life now!

155- Kauai the Cat

Sitting in a hammock
And thinking of Kauai

Of all the people who have been kind to me in my life
I think she has been the kindest

Looks into my eyes with those sweet, green, cat eyes
She'll always let me pet her
Always sits on my lap
Her body so warm against mine
Her fur so soft
Never bothers me with meaningless words
But will sit quietly with me for hours if I like
She doesn't waste time over thinking
But lives spontaneously through the instinct, intuition and heart
The best way imaginable

In my mind, I can feel her cat whiskers against my cheek
For her, the simple moment of being together is enough
Her love feels unconditional

Only she knows
The true meaning of life:
To pet and be petted

156-
All Stories Are Just That!

157- Never Count Out Anybody

I remember once, years ago, when I used to work at a library in California, there was a young homeless man that would come in everyday. As the days passed, he began to look increasingly haggard and sullen. The clothes he was wearing became more and more ragged and torn. He was growing thinner and thinner until he had become skin hanging on bones. When he was gone for weeks, I assumed the worst.

Then one day he suddenly strolled into the library radiant and healthy, with a huge smile on his face, wearing a brand new suit and a top hat! I felt no need to try to understand the rational explanation for this miracle in front of my eyes, if indeed there was one. What I remember was the phrase that came clearly into my mind at that moment:
"Never count out anybody!" A lesson I never forgot.

158-
Belief Creates Reality

159- 4PM Sunday

Two ducks slowly paddle across the pond
A small group of cows look at each other with serene eyes
As they graze along its edge

Everything is sharp green
In contrast to the bright blue and white sky
And the deep soulful, earthy browns
In the tree branches, rocks and mud

A gentle wind inspires the fragile leaves

A jubilant dog
A Labrador and his owner
Play games with a tennis ball
In the green meadow
To the right of the pond
Upon the background of an unending horizon

The earth is a song of creation
Upon which all life sprouts

160-
Live Without A Future
Or A Past

161- River Of Consciousness

Here I sit at the seat of consciousness
It's been a long, strange, trip to the core
Digging in circles
'Til finally the heart melts through
And life is like a river

Come down and join me at the banks
And together we can watch it roll

162-

Stand still
And watch the world run

163- Thoughts

All the thoughts about your past are happening right NOW
All the thoughts about your future are happening right NOW
The present
This moment right here is impossible to think about.
Let me see you try!

164-

Always trust your intuition

165- California Freedom

California
So many songs and poems dedicated to you but I had to write one
more

Dear California

California Freedom

Why do you love me so much?
And why do I love you back
Like the bad girl downtown
Many told me not to spend time with?

Why do you drop sunshine on me like roses?
Why do drop clear, blue skies on me like blankets of love?
Why do you give me Redwood forests that make me look up and
praise the creator?
Why do you give me smiley faces and big, blue oceans?
And hilly, green coastlines with dancing sea lions, singing birds
and a heart that beats twice as loud when the clouds drift by like
Italian men on gondolas?
Why do you give me endless grapevines and open air?

From the Sierra Nevada to the San Francisco Coast
A California dream come true

Dear California
I want to thank you
For letting me be myself

166-
There is no use in pretending to be something you're not.

167- We Are the Energy of the Sun

In this galaxy
We are the energy of the sun
Floating around
Doing good
And having fun

168-
Trust The Intelligence Of The Heart!

169- True Humility

There is a big misunderstanding about the meaning of the word
humility
True humility does not mean assuming everybody else is better
than you and therefore letting them manipulate you in whatever
way they wish

True humility is the inner peace, freedom and joy that arises
when you embrace everything exactly as it is because you don't
know if it should be any different.

In this humility, there is an inner power that is tapped into which
cannot be comprehended by the intellect

170-
Follow Your Divine Bliss

171- Dentist the Menace

Mt. Diablo perched amidst the California blue sky
Shining across the summertime world like an August diamond
Clear as a crystal

Please, let me stop right here and die in the empty afternoon
summertime void
Let me die in to this moment
Let me die in prayer
In deep peace
At the feet of this glorious mountain

But no...
Time for my dentist appointment

172-

If you ever find another moment better than this one
Please tell me

173- Brown-skinned Woman

Brown Woman

Your grace is unparalleled
Your strength is beyond compare

Your beauty and joy shine forth through your eyes with pure
radiance

Your smile is soft
But yet says so much

There are a thousand stories
And a thousand generations
In the smile you carry

As I watch you walk across the crowded intersection
I see you are in rhythm with the entire universe

Where others hear noise
You hear music

You found God the one place no one could take it from you
Inside the chamber of your own heart

Through all the hardship and pain
You discovered who you really are

You discovered your confidence
Your strength
Your wisdom
Your beauty
Your laughter
Your soul
Which is not based on external factors
But comes from within

Brown-skinned woman

In you, there is a harmony and a grace many have never gone
deep enough to discover

Brown-skinned Woman
Big, brown eyes
Sensuous full lips
Skin full of vibrant colors of the earth and forest
Beautiful, natural frizzy hair
Tight bouncy curls
Wild and free
Pure smile
Big, round feminine hips

Brown-skinned woman
Rounded and full of soft symmetrical curves

You are beautiful just as you are
Don't let anybody tell you any different

Brown-skinned woman
This one's for you

174-
Make Your Life A Work Of Art

175- You Are the Blue Sky

There is an afternoon blue sky with white clouds floating through
it
The white clouds are your emotions, your thoughts, and your
experiences
They come and then they go
Appear and disappear
Amidst the vast blue sky
But they do not define you
You are the blue sky

176- There Is...

There is something
So magical
No one can speak of it by name
And yet every word
Ever uttered
Is a name for it

177- Beyond Fear

You're the other half of the sky
You're the other side of the galaxy

You're the red bursting sun
That is so beautiful I can't look directly into it
Just squint my eyes and smile

This melody continues to play through our hearts
We couldn't stop it now if we tried
There are no rocks left to hide under

We must face the truth
All that stands in our way is fear

We must stay focused on the prize
Face our tiger
In acknowledging the truth
There is always true freedom

178-
The Time On My Watch Says "NOW!"

179- Being in the Moment

I'm walking around
Sitting around
Biking around
Hiking around
Looking around
Working aound
Playing around
Laying around

And all the time my mind is going, going, going

Thinking of all the places I want to live
All the places I want to visit
All the things I want to do
And see
And be

And then she tells me she's pregnant
That was a surprise!

180-
SMILE!

181-
To Live Fully In This Moment
Is To Die Fully In This Moment

182- Clarity

Clear blue sky
Clear blue lake
Clear green grass
Clear white clouds
All thanks to a clear blank mind

183-
Share Your Gifts With Everyone!

184- The Miracle of Flight

Late afternoon Friday
How wonderful the moth is
Flying above the bushes

185-
The fastest path to spiritual growth is to always tell yourself the
truth

186- This Moment

This Moment Is A Small Treasure
And You Hold The Key

187- The Three B's

"Be Good
Be Kind
Be Healthy"
-Giovani Amor (my son) 5yrs old

188-
Life: A Serious Joke

189- Blaze of Glory

Surely
You've got a story
Even if the world
Wants to ignore ye

So many things in this world to do
So many fears to hold us back

But promise me one thing
Before you're underground on your back

You'll go out in a blaze of glory

190-

See ourselves as excitations in the mind of God

191-

You can't think of something
Until you think of it

So give me people a break!

192-

The past had the great religions
The future will have the greater religions

193- Anne Doesn't Want To Go To Heaven

Anne said she was a Christian because her parents were
Christians
And if her parents were Muslim
She's sure she would have been Muslim
But she wants to know what she would have been if nobody told
her anything
She told me her Aunt says to her, "Only Lutherans go to heaven."
Anne says to her, "If that's true, I don't think I want to go."

194-

"God Made 'Em So I Don't Grade 'Em"
-The Good Reverend

195- The Peace amidst the Storm

At sea today
Turbulent storms
With violent waves
Torrential downpours
Crackling thunder
And white lightning
But underneath
The ocean floor is quiet and still
And tomorrow the blue skies will return

196-

Progress comes through a shift in our present perception not in the future material world

197-

We're filled with so many ideas, preconceptions and expectations
But the truth is
We really don't know what is going to happen next!

198-

Life, and you yourself, are eternally mutating and evolving.
It's best to enjoy the process.

199- Western Magic

The American West
With its vast expanse
Is a breath of fresh air
Of freedom itself

With its miles and miles of open spaces
Its towering rugged mountains
Barren desert plains
Crystal clear lakes
And eternal blue skies
It is an inspiration to the human heart

Here I sit
Underneath a jagged mountain
That looks as though it was sculpted by God
As it cuts through a traversing cloud
And into the open blue sky with its snow-capped peak

And my mind says to my heart
"I could never create something like this myself"

200-
Nature: That which is without effort

201- Unexpected Presents

Life is filled with unexpected presents

I blew a snot in a tissue and forgot it there

Bobby picked it up to use it
He was disgusted

Life is filled with unexpected presents!

202- An Option or a Decision

Your choice

203- Fall in Love

Quiet mid-afternoon
In the middle of a soft
Sunshine-filled, Northern California October

I realize the person I have been waiting to meet
All these years
Is actually myself
And here I am
For the first time

Hi
How are you?

204-
Can you feel the intensity, the uniqueness of this moment?
Can you see that you have never experienced this moment before
And you will never experience it again?

205- The Gift

To see you
To listen to you
To smell you
To touch you
To hold you
To hug you
To kiss you
To taste you
To feel you deeply
To bring you the gifts of the sea
To pray for you
To read to you

To bow before you
To honor and serve you
To cherish you
To adore you
To caress and lick you

To bring you new information and knowledge
Wisdom
Beauty
Fulfillment

To bring you the passion
And also the peace

To bring you music
And the deepest of silence

To hold your hand
To walk with you underneath the quiet moon
To play with you in the open meadow

To dance with you
To eat with you
To love you

To bring you flowers and poetry

To walk with you in the Spirit
And taste your sweet sugary-honey
To smell the spearmint and jasmine in your garden

To inhale you deeply into my lungs
And breathe you back out
With every single breath
To recognize the divine in you
And therefore also in myself
In this moment, right here
Is a gift beyond imagination

206-
Money
Is funny
When you're on a date
With your hunny

207- Boy in the Tree

I see a boy by the pond
Standing in the branch of a tree
Sunny, Tuesday afternoon of California May

He jumps and shouts with joy
In an incomprehensible language

His father looks on with a serious face and says
"Be careful now."
And then continues worrying about his financial future

And then I realize that this world is the playground of the
children
The rest of us are just here to make sure they don't get hurt

208-
Fixed conclusions close the mind off to the present

209- Human beings

Human beings
We are a transitional species
Moving from animal to Spirit Animated
We are evolving into a new type of being
With a new mode of consciousness
New powers of perception
Creativity
Strength
Intelligence
Wisdom
And capacity for love and connection
Wonderful to be sharing the ride with you

210-
Let's take care of each other
We're all we have

211- On Cloud Nine

Here I sit on a rift of rocks
Like first class stadium seats
As I watch the big, puffy, white clouds with gray underbellies
Perched against their bright, blue background

I hear birds singing
See butterflies dancing

Bright little flower cups smiling
And I smile back

The sun warms my neck and back
The air is still, but succulent

A little flea flies in
He sits on my belt buckle
And together we daydream
As we watch the clouds of all sizes

They look like a family
Momma clouds
And Poppa clouds
Baby clouds
Funky rebellious teenage clouds
These clouds are very interesting
They don't concern themselves with glory or fame
They are not interested in money or material riches
They feel no worry or stress
They do not fret about how they'll be taken care of

They do not compare themselves or desire to compete with the
other clouds

They do not seek anything in return for floating
Or appear troubled in anyway

And yet they seem to have everything they need

The flea and I are both very impressed

212-
You should never explain a poem
But it always helps!

213- The Blackberry

In the marsh
With the long shadows
The bright sun shining on my face

In this moment beyond compare
I picked it
The blackberry

214- Love
Love is the answer to every question!

215- The Thank You Prayer

Thank you for the trees
Thank you for the difficult people in my life
Thank you for the color blue
Thank you for the shape of a dolphin
Thank you for the smell of hot pizza when it just comes out of the oven
Thank you for anyone who has ever insulted me
Thank you for smiling, laughing free-spirited children
Thank you for my elders, their wisdom and guidance
Thank you for tulips
Thank you for orgasms
Thank you for thunderstorms
Thank you for the pain I feel in my back
Thank you for women
Thank you for men
Thank you for small, quaint country towns
Thank you for the energy, the cultural diversity and richness of the big cities
Thank you for mountains
Thank you for China
Thank you for salt
Thank you for poetry
Thank you for slow-dancing underneath the moonlight
Thank you for round logs of dog poop in the sunshine
Thank you for anger
Thank you for pain
Thank you for innocence
Thank you for untrammeled joy
Thank you for touch and sensuality
Thank you for beautiful fruits and vegetables straight from the earth

Thank you for my body
Thank you for yours
Thank you for singing birds
Thank you for the menstrual cycle
Thank you for a million twinkling stars in the evening
Thank you for monkeys
Thank you for music
Thank you for sports
Thank you for faded blue jeans
Thank you for love
Thank you for hatred
Thank you for deep silence
Thank you for money
Thank you for brown bears
Thank you for paper
Thank you for the islands in the South Pacific
Thank you for those days when I didn't have a dime
Thank you for the ocean
Thank you for red salsa
Thank you for fear
Thank you for hope
Thank you for seashells
Thank you for hummingbirds stopping in mid-air to stare into my
eyes
Thank you for desire
Thank you for rainbows
Thank you for deep inner freedom
Thank you for attachment
Thank you for guitars
Thank you for seagulls
Thank you for soft skin
Thank you for earplugs
Thank you for the great artists
Thank you for dental floss
Thank you for the human voice
Thank you for deep sleep
Thank you for Autumn leaves and cool crisp Autumn nights
Thank you for sunsets
Thank you for our genitals

Thank you for strong flowing rivers
Thank you for green lettuce
Thank you for the lessons learned
Thank you for fields of wildflowers
Thank you for all the isolation and sadness I have felt in my life
Thank you for all the physical illness I have faced in my life
Thank for wild mountain honey
Thank you for the clouds
Thank you for apple juice
Thank you for the moon
Thank you for great friends
Thank you for lightning bugs and fireflies
Thank you for peace
Thank you for death
And the new life it brings

Thank You

Now write your own!

216-
When your intentions are clear
The details are easy

217-Like Cookies in Milk

The Small love is vanishing.
The BIG LOVE is coming down ...
Where did I go?
We are disappearing like cookies in milk

There is a huge fire that is burning and spreading all over the
world
Touch it and the ego slowly burns away

It's getting hot in here!

218-The Most Wonderful Person

The most wonderful person
Is the one you meet next!

219-Going Nuts!

I want something else
Not this pecan world of peanut breath

Not the backseat of this peanut gallery
I don't want to live with a bunch of nuts!!
I want a higher kind of hard-shelled seed

I want to walk down the clean streets of pistachio drive
I want to shake hands with a cashew

I want a house next to a walnut grove
And a walnut creek
And a computer store owned by a walnut geek

I want almond joy!

220-

Small things done well
Lead to large things done even better

221- Child Friendly

It's Tuesday afternoon
He's stressed out
He's wearing his business suit
It's hot outside

He hates his work
The mortgage is due
So is the car payment
His wife won't talk to him
His father is sick
A lot on his mind

He's walking back from his lunch break
Some kids are playing touch football in the grass
They ask him if he wants to play
To his surprise
Something inside of him quickly says, "Yes."

He takes off his sport coat
Loosens his tie
He hasn't done anything like this in many years

He's running
And chasing
And laughing

He is a kid lost in play
No time
No name

The game is coming to an end
High-fives all around

Walking back to the car
His face breaks out into a smile
Everything looks different
Work's not that bad after all

His father is getting better and stronger everyday
The car and mortgage payments will be in the mail by tomorrow
He'll patch things up with his wife tonight

222- The Cancerous Growth

There is a cancerous growth on the human body
And it's called our brain!

All this useless thinking will make you sick!
Take your mind and lay it down in the river somewhere
Let it float away
Take a deep breath
The heart will lead you back

223- There Is Only the Hummingbird

I am walking quickly
Thinking I need to get somewhere

Suddenly I see a hummingbird
Flying above the vibrant flowers

I stop in my tracks
And embrace the magic of this moment

Time stands still
And nothing else exists
There is only the hummingbird

224- Science

Elephant shit
Is Big
Compared to a mouse's

225- The Dusty Trail Of Tears

So many still searching for the Ultimate Freedom
Amidst the dusty trail of tears
Which so many have tread
For so many decades

You won't find it in the future
But in the dust below your feet

226- Risky Business

College Boy approaches College Girl:

College Boy: What's your major?
College Girl: I major in business
College Boy: What kind of business?
College Girl: None of yours.

College boy approaches another girl

College boy: What's your major?

227- You Are the Beach

You are the beach
Thoughts
Feelings
Actions
Let everything move in
And let everything move out
Like the tide of the ocean

228- The Ocean

The ocean
So large and vast
My heart yearns for the open and forever expanse of the great,
blue ocean

The ocean
Because it is limitless
Because it goes by its own time
Because it gently sways back and forth to its own private dance

The great ocean
Because it is constant and forever

With sun
The ocean

With moon
The ocean

With clouds
The ocean

With storm
The ocean
With wind

The ocean

When the ocean is still
I look into my reflection and see infinite possibility

I am inspired to think of large and wondrous things
Let all my cares and worries drown into that great, big sea of blue

Let me sit by you and daydream of foreign lands I cannot see
And may never see
But yet I am connected to
Through your gentle shores

Dear Ocean
As I watch you meet the majestic sky with love
As the seagulls smile down upon you with reverence and joy
As I feel myself slowly drift away in your tide

I decide I am going to write a message
And send it out to humanity
In a bottle today

Place it upon your shore
And let your current take it wherever you choose:

You are a single drop of seawater
But wherever you go
And whatever you do
You're always in the ocean

That's the message I want to send out

229-

I used to think so many things were impossible
I no longer think about it

230- Rubbing Elbows

Once upon a time
In a small town in America
There was an eccentric sage
Who taught the people many important life lessons, in unusual
ways, about the value of having a simple mind and stress-free
living

One day while walking through the park
A group of townspeople were shocked to find the sage
Sitting on a bench masturbating

The townspeople were stunned
"What are you doing?" They said in disbelief

"I am massaging my penis"
The sage replied matter of factly

"Why?" They said

"Well I could rub my elbow but this feels much better"

231-
In the beauty of nature
We see ourselves reflected

232-Inside the Flower Cup

Walking in the meadow today
The flowers in yellow and purple
Long majestic trees in various shades of green
I saw your face inside a flower cup
Your eyes blooming
Radiant and pure with natural delight
Your hands gently folded at peace in your lap

233- The Fine Print

A woman with a magnifying glass
Reads the newspaper
It's actually not all bad

234- Listen to Your Heart

When trying to make important decision in your life
Put your hand on your heart
Ask yourself the question
Be receptive and silent
Listen closely the response that arises
You know what to do

235-
The Answer is in your Heart

236- Swimming in Her Eyes

Her beauty shines across a room
When she enters it

Her body radiates with energy, light and joy
I could swim inside her eyes
They burn love holes in my heart
And the entire world can see right through me

She seems like a child from a far off star
Who landed on earth for a brief moment
And yet, is somehow one with us all

237-

What is my purpose?
To open you up to the miracle of Life

238- Wise Woman

Wise Woman
Strong Woman
Healer
Mystic
Mother
Daughter
Sister of the Vast Galaxy
Divinity Among The Divine
With music dripping from your soul like sweet Canadian maple
syrup
Today is like a bouquet of beautiful flowers
Let's smell them and take in their fragrance

239-
Whatever you can imagine
Are the building blocks for the reality created

240- Death Wish

He wants to accomplish nothing
He wishes to say nothing
He wishes to hear nothing
He wishes to be recognized for nothing
He wishes to earn nothing
He doesn't want to be remembered
He doesn't mind being forgotten
He is dead to egoic ambition
And yet more fully alive than ever

VI: Sunset

241- In the Twilight

Walking peacefully
In the twilight
I suddenly thought I saw you one time
It was many years ago
Or maybe it was yesterday
Or tomorrow
At the horizon where dream
And reality merge
And become inseparable

It was getting dark
Beneath the flame-orange sun
And above the fading green hills
I thought I saw you

You were completely free
You were smiling
Happy
Filled with the light of the coming stars
And the bright travels of the shimmering moon

I could feel you in my heart
And the future being pulled into the present

As the darkness set in
And the earth grew cool
I did not need a jacket

I fell asleep in the tall grasses
The light in my heart kept me warm throughout the evening

I woke up to the brightest new sun
Inside an unending field of glistening wildflowers

I thought I saw you there

242-Twilight in the Mountains

The clock still moves

In the ebb and flow
But here there is no clock
And time is not an issue

The sun falling pink
In a lazy, Spring, ocean sky
With waves of cloudy foam
In to the Mountain mist
Like a scoop of sweet strawberry ice cream
Slowly melting in to the jagged horizon

The city below is vibrant with restless activity
Like bees in a honey comb
I see them buzzing and flapping their wings

Here it's quiet
The city looks small
Like it's made of a somber Legos

The air is crisp, pure, clean and invigorating
I inhale deeply and take in the fragrance of the fresh pine-scented
breeze

A light snow begins to softly float from the heavens
Soft, rhythmic and slow
The snowflakes invite me into their graceful dance
Like ballet dancers falling to the bountiful earth
Moistening it with their soft wet kisses

Let's sleep here tonight and let the snow be our blanket

And if I never told you
You Are Loved
Tonight I'll write it in cursive in the stars for you
And have the birds sing it to you at daybreak

In the morning, let's eat breakfast

243-At the Horizon

Imagine the earth
As the real world
And the sky
As the dream world
I'll meet you at the horizon

244- The Price of a Good Sunset

Looking at the texture of these hills
I feel as though I found God

The way they cup and peak
And ebb and flow all along the valley

The grasses wearing their deep Spring green
With a touch of the Summer brown beginning to show by the old
oak trees
The hills lined with little, tiny, flower cups of all different colors
Violent, yellow, sky blue, reddish-pink, white
And every other color your heart can imagine

I hear the faint voices of children playing in the distance, in the
valley below
I hear the wind whistling through the trees
I hear moments of deep silence and stillness

I see birds I didn't even know existed
And could care less about knowing their names
Just to see them is amazing enough!

A big, black hawk glides by to whisper something in my ear

The sun at a ninety-degree angle in the sky
Casting shadows along the hills and behind the trees
Where young kids hide and giggle

The sun so big and bright
But they say it's just a star
I don't believe them
I think it's much more
His rays touch me and fill me up with warmth and love

I nod to the sun and say
"Thanks again for rising up this morning"

The Big Sun nods back
"You're welcome, but I just stand still.
You spin around me. I just watch and smile"
"When will the beautiful moon come on stage?" I ask

"In a few hours" He says with excitement
"She's completely full tonight you know, and ready to put on a
dazzling show. But first, I am going to put on a sunset
performance like you have never seen!
No ticket needed."

245- The Flow

Don't build a dam
Life flows like water

246- Over the Big Highway

Riding over the big highway
Make a left
Over the hill
Across the farm
Hit the peek
Look straight ahead
Just in time for the show

Big hot red sun slowly melts into the distant hills
I hear the birds sing the Friday Night Blues

It's mid-April
Love is magic

Admission is always free

247-
We come into life because we love stories and games

248- Simple

Blue sky
White clouds
Red-hot, Firebird Sun
Sitting low but can still feel the warmth of her love

Food cooking on the stove
My baby's got a certain gleam in her eye
I look up and see a hint of the coming stars in the sky
And the moon ready to come out and play
And I realize
Life is complete just as it is

"Thanks life
Just for life itself"
Those are the words that enter this open mind

I didn't ask for them to come
And I won't ask for them to go

249-
EMBRACE EVERYTHING!

250- Sunny Ocean Dreams

Tonight on the beach
As I get sleepy
From a hard day of shining my rays

I close my eyes
And peacefully melt into a vast ocean of infinite ease

The sun is getting sleepy

From a hard day of shining his rays
He closes his eyes
And slowly melts in to the bottom of the ocean

Underneath the tranquil ocean water

We are slowly melting in o each other's dreams

251-
When you are complete
There's less need to compete

252-The Light from My Heart

I am sitting inside the magical emerald forest
Quiet
Still
And at peace

Staring at the beauty of the leaves
And the singing birds

How the colors and shadows change with each passing moment
As the day shakes hands with the early evening

I have no flashlight
But the light shining
From within my heart
Will lead the way home

253-Questions and Answers

The question is more important than the answer
The question is open
The answer is closed
Stay open!

254- Creating Characters

You create a character
When you're a child
When you're young
And if people like it
You become it

Perhaps it's time to create a new character

255-
Life Is The Greatest Teacher!

256- Brave like a Soldier

Go in to love
Brave
Like a soldier on the battlefield

Go in to love
Like a child
Playing underneath the twilight sky
Covered in a blanket of soft pink clouds

Go in to love
Like music
Flowing
Melodic
Ebbs and flows
But always returns to the center

Go in to love
Like a boxer
Ready to take your best punch
Ready to be knocked out
Laid out on the canvas
But ready to get back up
Ready for victory
Ready for anything

Go in to it like a paintbrush
Dipping in to the most magical paint
Ready to leave the world of black and white
And enter the world of techni-color
The images of your dreams

Go in to love
Like an Olympic diver
Off the highest of high dives
Somersaulting toward the warm water

Go in to love

Like a scientist
A philosopher
A mystic
An anthropologist
An archaeologist

Go in to love
Taste it
Touch it
Smell it
Listen to it
See it
Squeeze it
Stroke it
Fondle it
Hug it
Kiss it
Massage it
Suck on it
Caress it
Dance with it

Let it move you
And guide you

Go in to love
Like a wild, shining emerald forest
Lay down inside its shade
Write a poem
And dedicate it to the stars

Go in to love
Like a vineyard
Taste it divine nectar
Drink its sweet wine

Go in to love
Like a new home waiting to be built
Go in to love

Drown in it like quicksand

Die for love!

If you die for anything
Die for love!
Die to be born a new
The peace that passeth all understanding

Go in to love
And return
To give life its meaning

257-
Images come and go
But the light remains

258-In These Final Hours

In these final hours
Before the decision is made
And the jury hands down its verdict

These words and the power of these words are all I have to prove
myself
In these final hours
And therefore the power of these English words is what I shall
use

In these final hours, the time has come to lay everything on the
line
We have come so far
So close

There is nothing I would not do to meet you right now
There is nothing in the world that is more important to me

No amount of money is too much
No amount of time is too little

There is no river I would not swim
No mountain I would not climb
No distance I would not travel

No risk I would not take
To look into your eyes

Mi comrade
Mi spiritual partner
Mi corazon
Mi alma
Mi amiga
Mi familia
Mi madre
Mi hija
Mi amante

To touch you gently
To embrace you
To feel your body gently against mine
To teach you
To learn from you

To hold hands along life's path
Amidst the Spring flowers
The Autumn leaves
The Summer twilight
And the Winter fire

To sing and dance together
To talk late into the evening
To lie underneath a million twinkling stars
To consider the Summer moon our friend
To dance in the tall green grass with the butterflies and the
bumblebees
To swim in the peaceful ocean
To bathe in the sea

To every day, fall deeper in to the energy of love that radiates out
to all beings
As the great teachers and prophets have always whispered to us

To consider the earth our rightful home
And visit all parts of it

To laugh
And cry

To read together
Write poetry
Heal the sick
Pray for the world
Paint pictures together
To be silent together

Before the earth was born

We knew each other
But we had to wait until this moment
I want to take care of you
Protect you
Help you along this great journey called Life

Eat beautiful, healthy food from the earth together
Raise our children together

Live together
Die together

Every moment is a miracle
If we have the eyes to see it

This moment right here is a miracle
Don't miss it

I too am the miracle you asked for
Brought into flesh and blood!

In these final hours
Don't miss me

259-
What's important is not what happens to you
But what you decide to do about it

260- True Security and Safety

Many people are looking for safety and security in this world.

What I have discovered in my life is that the deepest form of fulfillment
And the truest form of safety and security
Lies not in building status,
prestige,
and material accumulations

Not in institutions,
governments,
militaries
or corporations

But in
Family
Friendship
Community
and
Relationships

In these bonds, there is great strength, safety and security

In a word:

LOVE

261-
In this moment,
We are creating our future

262- At the Beach

I saw you walking along the beach
The sun slowly dropping in to the soft envelope where the ocean
marries the sky
Blazing a thousand colors in its wake
Which Mother Nature painted tonight just for you

The children running barefoot and playing gleefully by your side
in the fading sun

I saw you walking happy and at peace
Filled with light
As the moon and a dazzling million stars prepared to take their
turn
And bless your eyes and your heart with its evening magic

263-
You are in exactly the right place
At exactly the right time

264- Then the Oak Tree

Things did not go as planned
He walks back
Fast-paced and furious
Through the forest
Along the late afternoon trail
With the long shadows cast across the ground

He's walked this path a million times
He's lost in his mind
He's angry
Ill-tempered
Spiteful
Disgusted

Then the amazing oak tree
Shining in the twilight

265-It's Right Here!

Don't go from somewhere to somewhere
Here is where it's at!

266- He

He will not make you happy or be your "Prince in shining armor," as in the silly fairy tale girls are brought up with
Only the individual can make them self happy
He will be a partner you will grow together with spiritually and take in life's many wonders

He will teach you many things about life
You will teach him many things about life
You will share many things in common and also some differences
These will be complementary, fascinating and beneficial even though they may occasionally feel frustrating

Sometimes the lessons will be very challenging and difficult for you
Sometimes they will be very challenging and difficult for him
But you will love each other through it all
You will teach each other and learn from each other how to love
How to grow deeper in peace
You will learn and grow deeper together every day in peace and love and freedom
Together you will help the human species to find peace and joy
Your hearts will grow warm and tender when you look into each other's eyes

Together you will defend and protect the earth
Together you will breathe clean air and drink clean water
Together you will eat pure food of the earth
Together you will make sweet love
Together you will pray and meditate
Together you will take quiet walks through the forest in the twilight mist.
Together you will protect and help the small ones to grow strong and healthy, wise, kind and free
Together you will help many human beings as well as the animals and trees
Together you will walk the path in friendship and compassion

VII: NIGHT

267- Tree of Love

I heard you calling out my name
The divine essence incarnated
Sacred touch
Sweet quiet strokes in the late evening
The kids are asleep
And now we are like children
Playing in the Garden of Eden

The taste like honeysuckle
The smell of wildflowers in your early morning dew
In your eyes a million sunsets
When you move it sounds like music
Your touch sends electricity through the circuits in my spine

This moment is the only moment
This love is the only love
The higher power compels us both forward

I want to plant a garden with you
Watch your children grow
Bring you closer to the unreachable perfection

In this deep peace and stillness between our hearts
Therein also lies the passion

Tonight you are the rich fertile soil
And I'm planting the seed
That will form deep roots

268-
Dream
The Sweetest Dreams
And see if they come true

269- The Moon

When I was young
The moon
When I am old
The moon

When I am awake
The moon

When I am asleep
The moon

When I yell
The moon

When I scream
When I cry
The moon

When I laugh
When I love
The moon

When I see the face of God
The moon

When I dance around the room
The moon

When I howl

When I shout for joy
The moon

In Tokyo
The moon

In Dallas Texas
The moon
In Pittsburgh, Pennsylvania
The moon

San Francisco
The moon

In Mexico City
The moon

In Rome and Venice
The moon

In Cairo and South Africa
The moon

Beyond the Great Wall of China
The moon

In India
The moon

In 1949
The moon

In 2000 BC
The moon

On Mars
The moon

From a far-off star
The moon

In my mind
The moon

In your dreams
The moon

Reflected upon a still lake in January
The moon

Under the ocean
The moon

Upon the seven seas
The moon
Reflected in your lover's eye
The moon

On the day of your death
The moon
On the day of your birth
The moon

In the falling snow
The moon

Amidst the thunder and lightning
The moon

In Iowa
The moon

In Thailand
The moon

In Sydney, Australia
The moon

While making love
The moon

In Paris, France
The moon

In Moscow
The moon

In Baghdad
The moon

In Tel Aviv
The moon

In photographs
The moon

On Television
The moon

Reflected in the mighty Mississippi
The Tigris and Euphrates
The moon

In Palestine
The moon

In the forest
The moon

For murderers and thieves
Sinners and saints
Rich and Poor
The moon

When you think it's over
The moon

When you're sure it's just beginning
The moon

On the radio they sing about it
At night we talk about it
In solitude, we look up and wonder about it
Old poets write about it
The moon

Before the homosapien
The moon

Before the dinosaurs
The moon

When your grandchildren are all grown up
The moon

In war and peace
The moon

In the rumblings of the urban streets
The moon

In the back country roads
The moon

In the mountains
The moon

In the islands
The moon

On the quiet farmland
The moon
For every race and ethnicity alike

Boy and Girl
Gay or Straight
Thin or large
Tall or short
The moon

Sometimes I can feel the moon inside my own heart

Anytime
The moon

270- When I Cry

When I cry I like to let the tears run down my face
So people can see what a real man looks like.

271- Journeying to the Stars in an Old Wooden Boat

I spent my life journeying to the stars in an old wooden boat
Pushing my oar with great effort and vigor
Shimmering
Glimmering
Twinkling
I went without water and food
Rowing on fatigued and weary
When suddenly I realized
These stars I was chasing
Were not stars at all
But merely the reflection of stars
In the tepid river

Then I looked up...

272-
Like a Garden
All things grow with LOVE

273- The Music of the Future

The music of the future
It sounds like it's coming from another planet and yet
paradoxically, like you've been familiar with it since the
beginning of time...
It draws on the best rhythms and melodies from all continents
and cultures throughout history bringing them together in a stew
yet to be tasted, and new spices are added as well...
It is holistic and integral, touching you in all 7 chakras, from the
crown chakra all the way to the root chakra, bringing about a
profound degree of transformation and transcendence...
It transports you somewhere else beyond this earthly dimension
and when you return you are different than when you left...
Never quite the same again...
It reminds you who you really are...
It touches your spirit and you begin to recognize yourself in
every sound, every note in the universe...
Universe means one song

It's healing
Righteous

It opens you up...
Seeps into your pores
Reminds you of the importance of LOVE
The Heart
The journey of life
And the Peace of the Soul

The beginning is not really the beginning
And the end is not really the end

Just ongoing chapters and verses that float through the sky like clouds....

There is always a level of spontaneity and improv to this music
and yet a familiar rhythm
Whose roots run deep in our collective tribal DNA

It reaches for the sky
But is rooted in the earth

It embraces all parts of ourselves
The spiritual
And the primal
The Past
And the Present
And summons in to Being the rhythms and cultural movements
yet to come...

You know that magical state of consciousness right before you
fall asleep? Sometimes you can hear it there...
I'm getting sleepy...
Sing me a lullaby

274-
Use your brush
Paint This World The Most Magical Colors

275- Reflecting Upon What I Do

Reflecting this evening on one of the things that's most important in what I do
It is to cultivate the power of the imagination and vision
To be able to take a human being in and see what they have not yet become
But what is waiting to arise within them
To hold that vision and never waver from it
Even if they themselves cannot yet see it
I see it!
I see the beauty in them

To be able to see what is not yet real makes it real

To do the same with a moment, a garden, a tree, a child,
The New Day...

Who are we really?
We are the creative energy!
Life Artists!
This life can be our canvas

Creating this life and this world
This moment
And all our relationships
Large and small

But first, we must hold the vision
The dream
Harness the incredible power of the imagination to see as real what does not yet exist

In doing so we then dream it into being each and every moment

Starting right now

276-
There are no friends
There are no enemies
There are only teachers

277- I Saw You Last Night

Last night
In the garden
In the sunshine
In the mist and Shadow

In the forest
In the leaves and berries

In the jungle
In the palms and tigers

In the ocean
In the jellyfish and dolphins

In the beach
The sand
And shadows

In the mountains
Amidst the valleys
And the snow-capped peaks

In the rain
The puddles
And the quiet sound of the rain on the tin roof

In the snowfall
Bright white and fluffy
Floating down gently
Each snowflake unique

In the storm
The Eye of it
The lightning
And the thunder

In the desert
Open, Wild and Vast
With a Dazzling Sunset

In the Night sky
Mercury
And Pluto
The Moon
And a Billion stars

In the midst of the changing forms and landscapes
I saw you
Sitting cross-legged
Quietly and still
With your eyes closed

278-
The night sky is filled with many stars
Choose one that twinkles!

279-With the Night Vision

With the Night Vision

Heaving
Cold hands growing warmer

Swimming in and out of each other like schools of fish

Dreaming of the Ocean
Bathing in the Big Blue Open Sea

In the early silence of the twilight morning
Washing our hair underneath a Warm Costa Rican
Waterfall

Or maybe it's Hawaii
Or amidst the primal drumbeats and rhythms of
Africa - The Motherland
Or the remote beaches of Nirvanic Thailand

Or maybe it's Eden
A world of dreams and imaginations
We visit together in the late evening
In the 5th Dimension

Big Soft Red Hearts emanating from the interplay of our auras
entwining
And floating up in the sky like Love Bubbles
Transparent red heart balloons emitted into the Tropical sky

We sleep together underneath the stars
We eat coconuts
And bananas
Mangoes
Pineapples
And dates
Handfeeding each other from the nearby trees and foliage

The kids laugh and play all day
Barefoot and free

No clothing necessary

Don't kiss me
Or you'll kiss yourself
With the night vision

280-
What I am really doing
Is creating a new dimension of reality

281- Whole Moon

Nightfall
Dusk
Dark
Big
Golden-yellow
Crater-filled
Auspicious round moon
is rising over the dark horizon of the distant hilltops
Like a yellow king slowly rising to take his throne
Perched high in the twinkling, black sky
Of dazzling stars
Both near and far

A gentle breeze makes soft harmonious music
As it rustles mid-September harmonies with the leaves and
branches
Outside my 9PM window

I take one last glimpse of that moon
Now a vast quiet fills the room
Engulfs me
And makes me whole

282-
Excitement and anxiety are the exact same energy channeled in a
different way

283- Little Luna

Little Luna
She can move mountains with simply a smile

Like a wild sunflower
Let her free
Let her go
Let her run wild and naked in the Spring meadow
Her soul shining unfettered
And filled with joy

Let her sun beam down without clouds

The great ones cannot be tied down for long
Let's call her Luna
Let her roam the earth, freely and nomadically
Like a divine prophet

Leave her free to embrace entire world
Too wonderful to be bound

Let her bounce to the beat of her own drummer
Let her dance freely by the oceans and rivers
Let her swim where she chooses
Fall out of trees and get bruises
Paint the walls with red mooses
Let her cry when she loses

She wants to roam free in the wide-open fields
With the blue, skies above
She has no need for chains or fences

She wants to sail on a ship out at sea
Sleep in the open desert, under twinkling, blue stars

Ride the rails
Hitchhike through strange lands
Let her grow up free

Don't try to mend her
Or bend her
The way you like best

She wants to be in the big, jagged, snow-capped mountains at
night
Where no one but the birds can touch her
She knows her path
She knows what she feels in her heart

Trust her
Support her
And she will grow up
Strong, Smart and Beautiful
Intuitive and brave
With a free spirit
And love in her heart
Quick to smile and laugh

Easy to be with
But always hard to leave

284-
All morality can be reduced to one simple commandment:
Be Honest with yourself

285- The Starlight Dream

I want to tell you something about my life
I am a young poet who's fallen in love with the night sky

I dreamt of the early evening Summer sky
Brilliant and dazzling
And it woke up true

I dreamt of floating from star to star
And singing a song
For each star I visited
Dignifying each in all its glory

Sweet and soothing melodies emanating from my lips
Encouraging and inspiring each star to shine a little brighter
For my fellow human beings
So that they can see them in the early evening
When the lights are low
The air is still
And the crickets are singing

And make a wish upon them
For a greater life
And a greater world
That was my dream

286- Eyelash Moon

In the evening
The moon is a sliver
It sits in the sky
Like a long, curved eyelash
Of a large, beautiful, silver-haired Goddess
Don't blink!

287- The Mystic

The spiritual path of the Mystic is the most difficult path to explain
Is it even a path?

The Mystic leaps backward in to the sea of unknowing
They contemplate a life that cannot be put in to words
They come to live a life that cannot be put in to words
And life that cannot be justified or explained
But simply looked upon with awe
Thus to the others, and even to themselves, they becomes as
 incomprehensible and wondrous as the night sky

288-
Do you believe this moment is a miracle?

289- Let This Poem Be My Body Tonight

These are not mere words
These are droplets of rain in the Amazon jungle
White snowflakes at dusk in the painted desert
Rays of sunshine bouncing off urban streets
Ocean mist floating over Hawaiian palm trees
Snow-capped mountains no one would ever dare to climb
But just gaze upon in wide-eyed wonder
Flower petals of many colors floating down across Spring
meadows
Let this poem be my body tonight

290-
Day dreams
Are just like night dreams
But better

291- Shooting Stars

Shooting stars falling through the vast, open, night sky
Here for a moment and gone the next

Everything comes and goes like smoke
An eternal play of mirrors

Our mysterious, divine essence
Illuminated in a million different changing shapes and forms
Including yours

292-
The more clearly we realize our intentions
The more clearly our intentions become realized

293- Searching For the Missing Piece

Cries from the mouths of the discontent
Not realizing we are in a garden filled with the sweetest berries

We shout with the heartache of pain and suffering
While our very shouts are golden

We cry and sob throughout the cold, black night
While all the while the gentle moon smiles down upon us
Like a mother's love
A warm, soft blanket from childhood

We tear and rip at our own flesh with anger
While all the while, our own spirit animates it
With the shine of God's diamond

Inside every tear that falls from our cheek
Love waits for us with open arms

Find God within your own being
Wasn't it there all along?

294- Tonight

I saw God tonight
I didn't have to look too far

295-For Aleah

Last night
In the evening
The stillness before dawn
Amidst a billion twinkling stars
In the shadows
I saw you and a small kitten smelling a flower
In the fragrance of that flower
Exists the entire universe

296-
All Is The Self

297- It's Only Natural

Nature is the most powerful force in the universe.
It is energy undivided.

Remember the messages of our ancient Sages,
Those incarnated as both male and female,
Throughout all cultures, places, and times

You ARE nature!
And the same energy that courses through the solar system
Makes the rain fall
The green grass grow
Strong winds blow
And volcanoes erupt
Also courses through your veins
Has been intimately involved in the evolution of your brain
The feelings in your heart
And every single thought you think

It masquerades as the one who wrote these words as well as the
one who is reading this sentence right now

You,
Whoever you are,
And whatever you have or have not done,
Are always and forever
One with this energy
And nothing you can do, bad or good,
Will ever change that

This is the Good News
The true salvation
And the ultimate enlightenment

This moment,
The power and flow of nature resides inside you and all around
you
And all things are possible

Look up into the sky tonight and see yourself twinkling
Are you starting to understand why I say you are beautiful?

298-
Life is a river
Let's watch it roll

299- The Whole World Is My Lover

In the silence
In the evening
A thousand stars sparkling in the sky
The yellow moon hangs like a fishhook

Walking the streets at night
The whole world is my lover

300-

The Future is here
It's about to introduce itself
Make a good first impression!

301- The One Heart Community

In this One Heart Community
We are Co-creating

Together we dance

We breathe in Love
And breathe out Love
Like inhaling
And exhaling
The waves of the Ocean

302-

If you don't like this feeling
Just wait for the next one!

303- The Dancer

In the shadows
She moves
With grace and clarity to the music

An audience of ONE sits in quiet gratitude

Intent
Content
Her light
Her happiness
Fills the room

She is a star
Casting light down to the earth
And filling it with melody

Dancing among us
Playing among us

Enchanting us
Enticing us
Stoking our fires
Lighting up our hearts

Just walking across the room
She is rhythm and melody
Flowing
Present
Awake
Alert
Attentive
Aware
Emanating the beauty of the ages

She is the mother
The daughter
The sister

The lover

She is the performance
And I am the applause

Does the music move her
Or does she move the music?

304-
Good relationships are like good jazz
You never quite know where it's going
But you're confident it's going to be somewhere beautiful

305- The Silent Gateway

No Barriers
No Boundaries

You are that
Of which I cannot describe

I am that
Of which you cannot understand
No fence
This is the Silent Gateway

306-
Suffering Is Just A Call To Attention.

307- Death Dream

In my dream tonight I died
And before the death, I realized that life itself was a complete
dream
That the appearance of different people in my life
Was really just the appearance of myself in many different forms

All the schisms and divisions
Interpersonal conflicts
I was actually creating
I was really doing to myself
They were actually within me
And being projected outward
I felt a sense of sadness and regret and died
I knew that I would have to go through the game of life
Over and over again
Unending
Until I ended the schism and division between these different
aspects of myself
And came to complete peace with that which IS
With myself in all its manifestations
I knew that was my purpose
Our purpose

I woke up
Grateful for the dream
Grateful for Life
Understanding its purpose

308-

Hell is just a place we came from
Heaven is just a place we are going

309- Looking up at the stars

I often look up at the stars
I think of how tiny they look in the sky
I think of how in reality they are thousands and thousands of
times bigger than the earth
And then I think of unbelievably, inconceivably small we are
How inconceivably minute our little tiny minds are in this vast
and open universe

310-

Look at everything with the wonder of a child

311-A Place Called Understanding

In the quiet evening
When all is dark
Let us take each other's hands

I won't lead you
And you won't lead me

But let's move forward together side by side
Taking each step together, slowly,
And only when all agree to take it

Let's move forward with the same interest
The same intensity
The same love
And together may our perspective widen
Our hearts deepen
As we come to a place called:
Understanding
Together, beneath the vast moonlight

312-

It's not important if people love you
It's only important that you love them

313- Fire Light and Moonshine

It's nighttime
And we're sitting around the fire

We are all together
There is goodwill and cheer

Stimulating conversation
Poetry and music
Romance and Love
Jokes and laughter
Singing and dancing
Peace and passion

Our hearts are serene
There's no need to get drunk or high

Because tonight
Our hearts are on tap
And constantly being refilled
We are drinking moonshine
Straight from the sky

314-

There are few things more fulfilling in life than making new
friends

315- The Torch

I saw a sea of humanity
Moving toward the light
I saw you carrying a torch
Helping to lead the way

316-
Life Artists Do It For Love

317- The Song of the Evening

This evening there is music...

When I am quiet
I can hear it
The sweet melodies
The soft rhythm
Listen close
I am singing to you

318-
Your spirit is that which is timeless and spaceless

319- Choices

Choices

They offered him many things
money
fame
girls
sex
riches
diamonds
cars
houses
status
class
salary
prestige
property
power
comfort
and
security

He chose Freedom
And disappeared into the night

320-
Life is just a flash of images
Take a picture!

321- Smile for Me

I would like to see you smile
I am smiling right now
And when I smile
I hear the stars singing
And the drifting clouds
Are like pillows
Ready for me to sleep on

But when I see you smile
The music sounds even louder
And more beautiful
And the pillows are even softer

Smile for me please

322-

Listen to involuntary thoughts as if they were the sound of rain

323- Hide and Seek Moon

I am in a rush
Trying to get where I'm going

Suddenly I see it
The Moon

Peeks out from the clouds
And smiles at me
With its shimmering magic

I tell the moon to close her eyes
And count to ten
It's my turn to hide!

324-

To what extent can my brain be my heart's soldier?

325- Little Lanterns

Ambling home
In the quiet evening
And the crisp country air

The lightning bugs and fireflies
Are here to lead the way

326-

Everybody wants something
But who wants this moment?
This moment is not a thing.

327- May We Dance

This life can be difficult and challenging

When life gives us noise
Let's turn it into music
And dance to it!
In the still, cold, shivering night
Underneath the moon
With our hearts warm and close to each other
Let's dance!

328-
There is only ONE.
And that one is YOU!

329- With My Head to The Pillow

My head falls to the pillow
A million thoughts scurry across my brain
They bounce and fly in all directions
Until they return to the same place
From which they came

As the minutes pass
My mind becomes calmer
And I start to slowly drift into another world

I can no longer hear
I can no longer smell
I can no longer taste
I can no longer see
I can no longer feel
But still, I AM

My body is a memory
Though even memories no longer exist

My soul is flying through the dream world
To a zillion places I come and go

The ocean of consciousness scurries across my brain

I see heaven
I see hell
I see people known and strange

I visit other dimensions
I visit Jupiter
The moon
The twinkling stars
Black holes
And all spots in between

I ride in spaceships
I make love to beautiful woman
I fly through the air without wings

I can jump a million miles
And swim a million more

I talk to animals
And circus clowns that ride in flying saucers

I am shot but I am healed
I am killed and yet I live again

Then my eyes open
My head lifts from the pillow
And for short while
I am stuck inside this body again

330- Life Lessens

Think Less
Talk Less
Do Less

Be More
Feel More
Love More

331-
Before the universe existed
Life was a lot more boring
Do you remember that?

332- The New Cyber Tribe

"When the earth is ravaged and the animals are dying, a
new tribe of people shall come unto the earth from many
colors, classes, creeds, and who by their actions and deeds
shall make the earth green again. They will be known as
the warriors of the Rainbow." -- Old Native American
Prophecy

I feel this prophecy coming to fruition in our
generation as this new Global Rainbow Tribe is slowly
awakening, and becoming aware of each other from all parts of
the globe.
The exciting new mode of communication that is most
facilitating this change is the internet and we are just at the
beginning stages of what its full potential shall be...

Many of us from around the world have felt this prophecy
in our hearts. We are using popular social networking sites and
our own self-made websites everyday to fulfill the prophecy and
further awaken spiritual consciousness in the human being:

To bring into awareness
The oneness of life and consciousness.

We do come from many different, nations, cultures, creeds
and colors from around the world and are coming together
online as a new global tribe to create a world of consciousness,
hope and beauty

To share, learn and grow together,
To inspire, empower and support each other on this path.

We truly are the ones we've been waiting for.

333- Endings

Every ending
Is also a new beginning
May the Big Glow fill your heart

Keep going!

www.TheBigGlow.com

If this book has inspired you, I would love to continue sharing this journey with you in whatever ways you are called to share in it!

For Personal Life coaching sessions on living your personal life with meaning, purpose, and inspiration
These sessions have are incredibly transformative in people's lives and will be in yours as well

For information on upcoming speaking engagements, readings, retreats and sitting circles

For general feedback on this book and how it has impacted your life

For daily inspiration and insight

For more information about me, what I am up to, upcoming events, testimonials...and much more...

It's a lifestyle
It's a new dimension of living
And it's all right here:
www.TheBigGlow.com

Join me... As we positively transform ourselves, and thus the world in the process.

About The Author

Father, writer, life coach, spiritual teacher, poet, philosopher, mystic, musician, singer, actor, dancer, athlete, comedian, entrepreneur and life artist.

At the age of 20 years old, Brian was suddenly struck by a mysterious, debilitating illness that lasted for years, leaving him in intense, daily, physical pain and too weak to effectively function in society. When no medical or other authority figure could explain the suffering that was happening to him, Brian made it his life commitment to search for why we suffer.

What began was over 12 years of committed, serious inquiry, study and personal application into the fields of spirituality, religion, psychology, sociology, cosmology, ecology, health, arts, science, yoga, as well as the core of the enlightenment and self-realization teachings.

After leading a quiet, simple life for over a decade, Brian now feels a passionate calling to share his discoveries with those who are ready and interested.

Made in the USA
Lexington, KY
17 December 2010